T0358347

Cambridge Elements ☰

Elements in Pragmatics
edited by
Jonathan Culpeper
Lancaster University, UK
Michael Haugh
University of Queensland, Australia

SPEECH ACTS

Discursive, Multimodal, Diachronic

Andreas H. Jucker
University of Zurich

Shaftesbury Road, Cambridge CB2 8EA, United Kingdom

One Liberty Plaza, 20th Floor, New York, NY 10006, USA

477 Williamstown Road, Port Melbourne, VIC 3207, Australia

314–321, 3rd Floor, Plot 3, Splendor Forum, Jasola District Centre,
New Delhi – 110025, India

103 Penang Road, #05–06/07, Visioncrest Commercial, Singapore 238467

Cambridge University Press is part of Cambridge University Press & Assessment,
a department of the University of Cambridge.

We share the University's mission to contribute to society through the pursuit of
education, learning and research at the highest international levels of excellence.

www.cambridge.org
Information on this title: www.cambridge.org/9781009532969

DOI: 10.1017/9781009421461

When citing this work, please include a reference to the DOI 10.1017/9781009421461

First published 2024

A catalogue record for this publication is available from the British Library.

ISBN 978-1-009-53296-9 Hardback
ISBN 978-1-009-42149-2 Paperback
ISSN 2633-6464 (online)
ISSN 2633-6456 (print)

Speech Acts

Discursive, Multimodal, Diachronic

Elements in Pragmatics

DOI: 10.1017/9781009421461
First published online: June 2024

Andreas H. Jucker
University of Zurich

Author for correspondence: Andreas H. Jucker, ahjucker@es.uzh.ch

Abstract: This Element outlines current issues in the study of *speech acts*. It starts with a brief outline of four waves of speech act theory, that is, the philosophical, the experimental, the corpus-based and the discursive approaches. It looks at some of the early experimental and corpus-based methods and discusses their more recent developments as a background to the most important trends in current speech act research. Discursive approaches shift the focus from single utterances to interaction and interactional sequences. Multimodal approaches show that the notion of 'speech act' needs to be extended in order to cover the multimodality of communicative acts. And diachronic approaches focus on the historicity of *speech acts*. The final section discusses some open issues and potential further developments of speech act research.

Keywords: speech acts, research methods, discursive analysis, multimodality, diachrony

ISBNs: 9781009532969 (HB), 9781009421492 (PB), 9781009421461 (OC)
ISSNs: 2633-6464 (online), 2633-6456 (print)

Contents

1 Introduction: The Philosophical Foundations   1

2 The Empirical Turn in Speech Act Studies   8

3 Corpus-Based Approaches   17

4 'Is That Supposed to Be an Insult or a Compliment?':
Discursive Approaches   26

5 'He Gave an Apologetic Shrug': Speech Acts
and Multimodality   35

6 'O, Cry You Mercy, Sir; I Have Mistook': The Diachronicity
of Speech Acts   45

7 Open Issues and Outlook   54

Data Sources, Corpora and Dictionary   60

References   61

1 Introduction: The Philosophical Foundations

In the first section, I describe the rationale and structure of the Element. It is based on a careful look at research issues and methods and how they have developed in recent years. In order to contextualise the recent developments, this section provides a brief outline of the philosophical foundations of speech act theory and gives an outline of the four waves of speech act theory. The first wave of philosophical approaches started with the work of the language philosophers Austin and Searle and their interest in the pragmatic nature of individual utterances. This work inspired the empirical approaches of the following three waves. The second wave was interested in how different groups of people produce different speech acts and relied mostly on experimental approaches including discourse completion tasks, role plays and, more recently, perception experiments. The third wave switched from elicited to already existing data and searched for specific speech acts across large corpora. The fourth and most recent wave focuses on speech act sequences and the interaction between speakers and listeners in local contexts.

1.1 Setting the Scene

Speech acts have always been a central concern for pragmatics. In fact, they were one of the distinctive features of the discipline when pragmatics established itself as an independent field of study back in the middle of the last century. At that time, linguists were mainly concerned with the structure of words, phrases and sentences with little concern for their uses. But the early pragmaticists wanted to know how language was actually used to communicate or – to put it differently – how speech was used to act. For this, they relied on the work by the language philosophers John Austin and John R. Searle. Austin had developed a framework for the investigation of speech acts in a series of lectures delivered at Harvard University in 1955. These lectures were published posthumously in 1962 and they still provide a fascinating insight into the development of these new ideas as Austin developed them in the course of the lecture series. The starting point for his theorising had been the observation that many utterances could not in any straightforward way be classified as true or false because they were not used to report a certain state of affairs. Instead, they were used to do things. Hence, the programmatic title of his book *How to Do Things with Words*. Searle (1969, 1979) developed Austin's seminal ideas into a more elaborate and complex theory (see Section 1.2).

It is the work by these two language philosophers which inspired the first generation of pragmaticists to think and theorise about speech acts. But, as I will show in the following sections, the framework proposed by Austin and Searle provided some basic assumptions that persisted for much longer and still influence a considerable amount of analytical and theoretical work on speech acts within pragmatics. And this is why I would like to use the metaphor of waves to describe the development of speech act theory over the last half century or so. The wave metaphor has been used by other fields in linguistics, notably in sociolinguistics and in politeness theory. It helps to understand how new ideas develop on the basis of earlier thinking and how different theoretical perspectives blend into each other without hard and fast boundaries between them. The defining criteria of the waves that I will introduce in what follows are the basic assumptions about the concept under investigation, the research questions that are asked by the scholars working in the field and above all by the research methods that are employed for their investigation.

As a result of these changes, the notion of a speech act itself has changed somewhat. Initially, the term focused squarely on individual utterances that were used to perform certain actions, for instance how words can be used to greet, to promise, to apologise and so on. In more recent work, as I will show, the focus is regularly extended to include social and multimodal aspects. Sometimes speech acts are performed without any speech at all or with a combination of speech and gestures. A request to keep silent, for instance, may be performed by an appropriate gesture only; a greeting may be performed silently by a nodding of the head or a hand wave; and an apology may be performed by an apologetic smile. Such examples are the topic of Section 5. More recent research also focuses more consistently on the interactive nature of speech acts. The object of investigation is no longer a single utterance, but utterances in sequence.

Against such extensions of the analytical perspective, the term 'speech act' seems increasingly inadequate. Terms like 'communicative act' or 'pragmatic act' (Culpeper and Haugh 2014) may be more appropriate. The title of this Element still uses the traditional term, but in the following I will also use the term pragmatic act, especially when I want to draw attention to the multimodal aspects of what communicators do.

1.2 The Philosophical Beginnings of Speech Act Theory

Initially, Austin was interested in a small class of utterances that he thought behaved in a very special way. The philosophers at the time were mainly interested in sentences that could be classified as true or false and if they defied such classification, they were considered to be meaningless. But Austin identified a class of sentences that he called 'performatives' because in a very real sense they perform something and thus in some way change the world, as for instance 'I name this ship the Queen Elizabeth' or 'I bet you sixpence it will rain tomorrow' (Austin 1962: 5). He noted that in contrast with 'constatives' such performative utterances cannot be judged as either true or false. Instead they can be judged as more felicitous or less felicitous, depending on who uses them with what authority and intentions and in what context. By the end of his book, however, the two types of utterances, the 'constatives' and the 'performatives', were merged again because he realised that statements could be seen as the performance of an assertion. He also distinguished between three different aspects of each speech act, the locutionary, the illocutionary and the perlocutionary aspect, which describe the making, or pronunciation, of the utterance itself, its intended purpose and the effect it has on the audience.

In his book *Speech Acts: An Essay in the Philosophy of Language*, Searle (1969) set out to systematise Austin's insights into a larger and more coherent theoretical framework. He developed a set of felicity conditions that helped to identify specific speech acts. A request, for instance, must concern a future act of the hearer which the hearer might not have done without being asked and the speaker must have some interest that the hearer actually does what he or she is being asked to do. A promise, on the other hand, must concern a future act of the speaker him- or herself, which the speaker believes to be in the hearer's interest and which the speaker actually intends to carry out. If some of these conditions are not met, the speech act is not felicitous.

Searle identified these conditions as constitutive rules. They are similar to the rules of a game. Chess, for instance, consists of a set of very specific rules about the ways in which each of the six different pieces can be moved on the chessboard and what they are allowed to do. If people ignore these rules and move the pieces in different ways, they may be playing around with chess pieces, but they are not playing chess. Playing chess consists of following the rules. And in the same way, the felicity conditions constitute the act of performing a specific speech act. If someone says, 'I'll return the book tomorrow' and has no intention of doing so, he or she, in a crucial sense, has not felicitously promised.

Searle (1979) proposed a classification of five different types of speech acts. Representatives commit the speaker to the truth of what he or she says. This class largely corresponds to Austin's initial original class of 'constatives'. Typical examples are assertions. Directives are attempts by the speaker to get the hearer to do something. This can happen with more or less authority and includes such actions as begging, suggesting, advising, requesting or commanding. Commissives, on the other hand, commit the speaker to a future course of action as in promising or threatening. Expressives express the speaker's psychological state. Complimenting, apologising, thanking and congratulating are relevant examples. The final type of speech acts consists of declarations. They tend to rely on institutional contexts for their successful performance and effect an immediate change in the state of affairs, as for instance in a declaration of war, the christening of a ship or the appointment of a new committee member.

The groundwork provided by the language philosophers Austin and Searle was soon adopted into the new and emerging field of pragmatics and, in fact, one of the early textbooks in pragmatics, Levinson (1983: chapter 5), still provides one of the best introductions into this early version of speech act theory. For a more recent overview, the reader is advised to consult Culpeper and Haugh (2014: chapter 6) or Assimakopoulos (in press). Many of the concepts developed by Austin and Searle continue to be used as analytical tools up to today in spite of the numerous changes in research interests, methodologies and theoretical underpinnings.

Much of the subsequent work on speech acts inherited the original emphasis on the illocutionary aspect, that is, on the speaker and what he or she tries to do by uttering a string of words. This is usually called the illocutionary force of an utterance, but I prefer to follow a distinction proposed by Holmes (1984; see also Searle 1976) between the illocutionary point and the illocutionary force of an utterance. The illocutionary point refers to the function or purpose of a speech act, that is, whether it is an apology, a threat or a warning, while the illocutionary force refers to the strength with which the illocutionary point is presented, that is, whether it is a heartfelt and sincere or a casual and perfunctory apology, for instance. I shall come back to this distinction in Section 4.

1.3 The Four Waves of Speech Act Studies

The 1980s saw a growing interest in the newly emerging field of pragmatics with several important textbooks (in addition to Levinson 1983 mentioned in the previous section, for example, Leech 1983 or Green 1989) and the founding of the International Pragmatics Association. This was a time when linguistics was still dominated by formalist approaches that focused on linguistic structures and analytical tools that relied on native speaker intuition and invented sentences that were used as the basis for theorising. Against this background, pragmaticists began to ask questions about actual language usage. Speech acts were no longer seen as abstract entities that could be dissected with philosophical rigour into a set of constitutive felicity conditions. Instead, they came to be seen as performance phenomena whose realisation could be investigated across different groups of speakers. In the context of a move away from philosophical methods and introspection to more empirical methods, experimental tools were developed in order to collect data on how different groups of speakers produce specific speech acts. Section 2 will review some of these tools in more detail, in particular discourse completion tasks, role plays and perception studies.

In spite of this turn towards empirical methods based on systematic data elicitation and careful observation, many of the first wave assumptions about speech acts continued to inform these investigations. The focus continued to lie on individual utterances and on well-defined speech acts. The experimental designs were carefully created to elicit apologies, complaints or requests (Blum-Kulka et al. 1989, Trosborg 1995), for instance, and therefore the nature of these speech acts and what they were supposed to achieve appeared to be clear. What was at issue was merely their specific realisation.

In the 1990s, computers became more easily accessible. They were no longer restricted to IT departments and a few early pioneers in corpus linguistics, but they became available to more and more linguists. At the same time, more and more language corpora became available. With the *British National Corpus* for the first time a corpus became available that contained not only a few million words but 100 million words (see Landert et al. 2023). And this led to the third wave of speech act theory. It is probably fair to say that much of the early work in corpus linguistics was dominated by lexical and morpho-syntactic investigations. It took more time for these methods to be adopted for pragmatic entities. Early pioneers were Aijmer (1996) and Deutschmann (2003). With corpus-based approaches, the interest in speech act studies shifted from individual instances of performed speech acts to patterns of occurrence across large corpora. Some of these approaches set out to retrieve instances of the speech acts themselves while others focus on the expressions that are used to talk about them, the so-called meta-illocutionary lexicon (Schneider 2017, 2022).

The fourth wave brought a more radical shift away from Austin and Searle's original conception of individual utterances with specific communicative functions. Speech acts are now seen as fuzzy entities whose function is often negotiated in context ('Is that a request or a command?'). The focus, therefore, shifts from the speaker who performs a certain speech act to the interaction between two or more speakers. The illocutionary point of a speech act emerges in the interaction and depends on the degree of conventionalisa-tion of a specific speech act and the way it is (implicitly or explicitly) interpreted by the interlocutor(s). The perspective turns away from speech act labels assigned by the researcher on the basis of felicity conditions, so-called second order definitions. Instead, it focuses on the way the interlocutors conceptualise specific speech acts and deal with them, that is, on first order definitions. The speaker may feel the need to stress his or her sincerity and thus increase the illocutionary force of the utterance ('I solemnly promise that I will never . . .'), or the speaker may be urged to issue a particularly sincere promise ('Do you really promise?'). And speakers often negotiate the precise illocutionary point of a speech act ('Is that supposed to be an insult or a compliment?'). In the context of speech act research, the perspective on the interactional aspects in meaning-making were relatively new. In other fields, notably in Conversation Analysis and Interactional Linguistics, the focus on the discursive nature of language functions has a much longer tradition (see Couper-Kuhlen and Selting 2018 for an overview).

At the same time, the analysis of speech acts is no longer reduced to their verbal content. They are seen as multimodal communicative acts that can be performed by a combination of words, facial expressions and gestures. Such modalities can be combined or used individually. A simplified overview of the four waves can be found in Table 1. The categories across the four waves are not watertight.

1.4 Outline of the Element

This Element does not presume to introduce all aspects of the vast field of speech act research. For the more philosophical aspects of the field, readers are referred to its sister Element (Assimakopoulous in press). Instead, I will focus on what I see as particularly exciting developments in current speech act research, that is, their fuzziness, their multimodal nature and their historicity. And at the same time, I want to give a brief outline of how speech act research has reached this point by focusing on the developing research questions and research methodologies over the last few decades. In Section 2, I will review some of the relevant literature that introduced empirical methods into Austin and Searle's conceptualisation of the nature of speech acts back in the 1980s and 1990s, in particular the early methods of discourse completion tasks and role plays. Both methods have been criticised for some of their undoubted weaknesses, but they also have their strengths, and recent work continues to adapt and modify the methods in various ways. Section 3 provides an outline of four different ways of using corpus-based methods to investigate speech acts in large corpora. In Section 4, I will focus on the different ways in which pragmatic acts, as they will be called in the context of this section, can be analysed as fuzzy entities and thus no longer as theoretical constructs but as actual utterances whose communicative impact is negotiated (implicitly or explicitly) by the interactants. Section 5 will shift the focus to the multimodal nature of pragmatic acts and extend the analysis from the verbal aspects to gestures and facial

Table 1 Four waves of speech act research

	First wave: Philosophical	Second wave: Experimental	Third wave: Corpus-based	Fourth wave: Discursive
Timing	1960s/1970s	1980s –	1990s –	2000s –
Method	Philosophical	Empirical	Empirical	Empirical
Data	Introspection	Elicitation	Large corpora (incl. historical data)	Small corpora (incl. historical data)
Main focus	Felicity conditions	Speaker variation	Dispersion across corpora	Local contexts and the interaction between speaker and addressee
Definitions	Second order (i.e., academic)	Second order (i.e., academic)	Partly second order, partly first order	First order (i.e., participants' perspective)
Research questions	What are the essential features of specific speech acts?	What are the differences in the speech acts produced by different types of speakers?	Where and in what forms and functions are specific speech acts likely to occur?	How are speech acts co-constructed over several turns? How are they produced multimodally?

expression. Section 6 will then combine many of the elements of the previous sections and use them for an exploration of the historicity of pragmatic acts. The main question to be explored concerns their persistence or development in the course of language history. How did people in Anglo-Saxon England apologise, for instance? Or did they apologise at all? And how has this changed over the centuries since then? On a meta level, I will also be concerned with the analytical difficulties of tracing such developments. The final section of this Element will briefly discuss open issues and provide an outlook into future research opportunities in connection with pragmatic acts.

2 The Empirical Turn in Speech Act Studies

The early empirical work on speech acts set out to find experimental ways of eliciting specific speech acts in order to compare their realisation across different contexts and different groups of speakers. Initially, many of these approaches were based on an interest in the politeness potential of specific speech acts. Discourse completion tasks and role plays, for instance, were designed to elicit speech acts with specific face-threatening potentials in order to compare the strategies used by different groups of speakers when performing them. Other methods that were developed to compare speech acts across contexts were the creation of realistic situations or the observation of naturally occurring comparable contexts and ethnographic data collection methods. More recently, these methods have been extended to explore reactions and attitudes of addressees or bystanders when confronted with specific speech acts.

2.1 The Empirical Turn in Linguistics

The 1970s and 1980s saw a number of paradigm shifts that altered some of the basic tenets of linguistics in general and some of these shifts were foundational for the emerging field of pragmatics (see Traugott 2008: 207–10; Jucker and Taavitsainen 2013: 5–10). In the 1970s and earlier most linguists were interested in language as a coherent and homogeneous system. They were concerned with generalisations across entire languages and therefore ignored or backgrounded what they considered to be 'irrelevant deviations'. In their view, generalisations could only be accessed through the intuition of a native speaker while actual language production was considered to be contaminated by irrelevant factors, such as distraction, lack of concentration or tiredness of the speaker. The first wave of speech act theory clearly aligns with this kind of approach. The language philosophers Austin and Searle were concerned with generalisations about specific speech acts and they used the philosophical tools of introspection to determine the relevant sets of felicity conditions for specific speech acts.

However, in the 1970s and 1980s an increasing number of linguists started to explore the 'irrelevant deviations' of actual language use. They became increasingly interested in the heterogeneity of language and, as a result, the research methods changed from introspection to empirical investigation. The heterogeneity of language could only be investigated through careful observation of how people actually use language and how different groups of speakers systematically differed in their linguistic behaviour. The search for generalisations across entire languages shifted to searches for regular patterns in the variability of language. In the process, many linguists expanded from the core areas of linguistics, that is, phonetics, phonology, morphology, syntax and semantics, to sociolinguistics and pragmatics. 'What was marginal in the 1970s has come to be of central interest, above all pragmatics' (Traugott 2008: 207). The native speaker's competence was no longer an adequate basis for linguistic theorising. Instead, detailed transcriptions of everyday interactions, large corpora of conversational data and other texts and carefully elicited experimental data became the object of investigation.

It was against this background that the second and third waves of speech act theory emerged in the form of elicitation experiments and corpus-based research. These methods were used to show how different groups of speakers differed in the ways in which they produced specific speech acts. The following subsections briefly review some of these early studies, the criticisms that were subsequently levelled against them and some more recent modifications and adaptations of these methodologies.

2.2 Discourse Completion Tasks

According to Ogiermann (2018: 229), the discourse completion task is probably one of the most widely used methods of data collection in cross-cultural pragmatics as well as in interlanguage pragmatics. It facilitates the collection of large amounts of systematically comparable data across different groups of speakers. The best known and most influential study was the Cross-Cultural Speech Act Realisation Project (CCSARP) carried out in the 1980s by an international team of researchers under the lead of Shoshana Blum-Kulka (Blum-Kulka, House and Kasper 1989). They focused their attention on requests and apologies because these two speech acts were seen as good examples of face-threatening acts in the sense of Brown and Levinson (1987). Requests are impositions on the addressee and, therefore, threaten his or her negative face, that is, the wish of every person to remain free from imposition, while apologies acknowledge a minor or major misdeed by the speaker and thus threaten the speaker's own positive face, that is, the wish of every person to be liked by others. The project explored the different strategies used by speakers of Canadian French, Danish, German, Hebrew and three different varieties of English (American, Australian and British).

Discourse completion tasks typically consist of a brief description of an everyday situation, an utterance by a first speaker that makes a certain type of response highly expectable, an empty slot for the participant to fill in and a rejoinder by the first speaker which typically indicates that the speech act in question has been accepted. The participants are asked to fill in how they would react in this situation. Extract 2.1 provides a relevant example taken from Blum-Kulka, House and Kasper (1989: 274).

2.1　　In the lobby of the university library.
　　　　Jim and Charlie have agreed to meet at six o'clock to work on a joint project.
　　　　Charlie arrives on time and Jim is half an hour late.
　　　　Charlie: I almost gave up on you!
　　　　Jim: . . . .
　　　　Charlie: O.K. Let's start working.

In this situation, Jim is very likely to apologise for being late to the meeting. Such scenarios can be translated into different languages and therefore allow the researchers to quickly and easily collect large numbers of apologies by speakers across different linguacultures (cross-cultural pragmatics) or across native speakers and language learners (interlanguage pragmatics). The method also allows for systematic variations of contextual factors. The scenarios can be designed to involve friends or strangers as speakers. They can create symmetric or asymmetric relations between the speakers in terms of power, age, status and so on.

The methodology has proved to be popular because of the ease with which large amounts of contrastive data can be collected and the many ways in which contextual factors can be manipulated, but it has also been widely criticised. People write what they think they would say or perhaps even what they think the researcher would like to hear or what would make them look good rather than what they really say. They formulate these speech acts in artificial situations which do not have any real-world consequences. Some situations may be more or less realistic in different linguacultures and the available space provided for the written response may influence the length of the response. In general, written responses appear to be shorter than spoken responses and the design of the task allows for only one utterance. The follow-up by the original speaker indicates that no negotiations appear to be necessary. Whatever the response, the original speaker will accept it while in a real situation the original speaker may not be satisfied with the first response and ask for a 'real' apology (see

Section 4) or may initially refuse to carry out a request, and so on. In spite of these misgivings, discourse completion tasks are still being used, especially in the field of variational or interlanguage pragmatics. Anchimbe (2018), for instance, uses discourse completion tasks to compare offers and offer refusals in Ghanaian and Cameroon Englishes and Mascuñana et al. (2019) use them to investigate compliment responses by male and female Filipino ESL students. The methodology is often modified to account for some of the weaknesses of the original version, for example, the space limitation for the response, the modality of written responses for what would be spoken speech acts or restriction to one turn only. Their continued use is also justified on the basis of a more realistic assessment of their potential. They provide 'clues about the nature of communicative competence and, more particularly, the schemata underlying the production of all conversation' (Schneider 2011: 17). This view assumes that discourse completion tasks tell us what people think would be appropriate responses rather than what they actually say in such situations and it assumes that this is a strong point rather than a weakness. However, the jury is still out on the question of whether discourse completion tasks measure what they purport to measure or something slightly different.

2.3 Role Plays

Role plays were developed as a methodology for the investigation of speech acts in order to eliminate some of the weaknesses of discourse completion tasks while retaining their power for contrastive and experimentally controlled data collection (see Félix-Brasdefer 2018 for an overview). Like discourse completion tasks, they have been used widely in contrastive, interlanguage and variational pragmatics because of their potential to create contrastive settings and to control contextual variables. They generally ask study participants to enact a carefully constructed situation and to improvise how they would talk to each other if this were a real situation.

Félix-Brasdefer (2018) distinguishes between closed role plays and open role plays. Closed role plays elicit one-turn responses to a given situation and thus they correspond to oral discourse completion tasks. They often use elaborate multimodal prompts rather than just brief verbal descriptions and they provide the participant with the opportunity to give longer responses including oral features (prosody, hesitation, self-corrections etc., which are unlikely to be included in written responses).

In the open role plays, participants receive a situational prompt and are then asked to improvise the scene in the way that they would behave in a real situation. Extract 2.2 provides some example prompts used by Trosborg (1995: 388) to elicit apologies from Danish learners of English and control groups of Danish native speakers speaking Danish and English native speakers speaking English.

2.2　　A borrower (A) has failed to erase comments in the margin of a library book. The librarian complains.

It is A's birthday and he/she is giving a noisy party which lasts until late in the night. The downstairs neighbour complains about the noise.

Two friends share a flat and have agreed on a mutual cleaning arrangement. When A fails to do his/her share, the friend complains.

In all three situations, the apologiser, that is, participant A, is confronted with a complaint and has to apologise for what has happened. The three scenarios and many others like them, manipulate the role relationship between the apologiser and the apologisee (person of authority, stranger, friend).

Like discourse completion tasks, role plays have been criticised widely, but they also have their positive aspects. They are based on artificial situations in which the study participants pretend to complain or apologise. The performed actions do not have any real-life consequences. Some people feel uncomfortable if they have to play act in front of a researcher and a video camera, while other people may positively enjoy this and perhaps even exaggerate what they would do. It may be fun to shout at a noisy neighbour in the protected space of play acting and this may even be what the speaker would love to do in a real-life situation but would never dare. At the same time, some of the roles in these scenarios may be less familiar to the participants, if they have to play a police officer, a teacher or a professor, for instance. For this reason, Trosborg (1995: 144) distinguishes between role playing and role enactment. In role playing, the participants perform roles that they do not normally have in their real lives. They play someone else in a situation with which they may be less familiar. In role enactments, however, they play a role that is part of their normal life or personality in situations that are thoroughly familiar to them. In this way, the methodology tries to overcome some of the problems described.

On the positive side, role plays elicit interactions that are more natural than the written responses of discourse completion tasks. The outcome of the scenarios can be negotiated by the participants, who are not restricted to one single utterance. Similar to discourse completion tasks, they are a way of creating contrastive settings in which individual dimensions can be isolated (distance between the speakers, severity of the imposition and so on). They are a relatively easy way of collecting large numbers of responses by different groups of speakers of different languages, learner languages or different varieties of the same language. And they provide valuable information about stereotypical attitudes of what people believe to be appropriate reactions in the given scenarios, even if these reactions may differ from what people actually do in real-life situations.

In contrast to discourse completion tasks, however, role plays are generally more difficult to organise. Each interaction has to be arranged individually with every study participant, while discourse completion tasks can be distributed to large numbers of participants at the same time, be it on paper in a classroom, via an email distribution list or an online questionnaire. Moreover, role plays require careful transcriptions of every single interaction, while discourse completion tasks return responses that are already written out and need less processing before they can be analysed.

2.4 Comparable Contexts

The experimental approaches reviewed so far have often been criticised for their artificiality or lack of authenticity (see Jucker and Staley 2017 for a review). They either create contexts for study participants to produce certain speech acts or they confront study participants with different kinds of prompts to elicit evaluations of these prompts and thus they generally study what people think should be done rather than what people actually do in specific situations.

To overcome this problem, study designs have been created with a higher degree of authenticity by observing language behaviour in comparable contexts. Some researchers created comparable contexts for their participants while others made use of naturally occurring comparable contexts. Jucker and Smith (2003), for instance, asked pairs of study participants to watch the first half of a silent movie together, but only one of each pair watched the rest of the movie and then had to tell it to their partner. The resulting movie narratives were not entirely natural because they were recorded in a laboratory situation, but they were naturalistic in that they imitated a realistic task that the participants performed without having to act out an 'as if' situation. It allowed the researchers to contrast the communicative behaviour of native speakers of English and different types of learners of English. In a similar way, Szatrowski (2014) recorded so called taster lunches in which sets of three participants tasted a range of foods from Japan, America and Senegal and were asked to talk about their experiences, and again, different groups of speakers could be compared in their choice of linguistic strategies to talk about food. These studies did not focus explicitly on specific speech acts but on a range of communicative tasks that the researchers knew in advance would be part of the chosen communicative settings of movie narratives or taster lunch conversations. Such settings, therefore, provide a somewhat more authentic context than role plays because they avoid the enactment of 'as if' situations.

Other researchers made use of naturally occurring comparable situations, such as service encounters, which generally have a relatively conventionalised structure and a limited range of speech acts that can be expected to occur within them. Félix-Brasdefer (2015), for instance, used service encounters in supermarkets located in Mexico and the United States of America in order to compare the issue of politeness across the two linguacultures. In the process, he analysed opening sequences as well as thank-you exchanges, both of which are highly expectable in the encounter between a shop assistant and a customer. Nilsson et al. (2022) used service encounters recorded in Sweden and in Finland to investigate greetings. They investigate not only the different localities but also other speaker demographics, such as gender and age, to account for the variability in the data. Rüegg (2014) and Staley (2018) used data collected in three sets of Los Angeles restaurants to investigate how waiters in different socio-economic contexts interact with their clients, in particular how they offer food choices and how they respond to thanks. In all these studies, the analysis focuses on specific speech acts that regularly occur in these contexts and can, therefore, be compared across the different samples collected for the study.

One drawback of this method consists of the fact that, like the experimental laboratory studies, prior informed consent is required from all the people who take part in these service encounters and, therefore, they are never entirely free from the observer's paradox. The researcher cannot observe communicative behaviour that is not being observed. Participants are always aware, at least to a certain extent, that they are being recorded, even if they get distracted from the recording situation in the course of the interaction, and thus their behaviour may deviate somewhat from what it would be if it were not being observed and recorded by a linguist.

2.5 Ethnographic Studies

Another way of reducing the impact of the observer's paradox and increasing the authenticity of the data consists in an ethnographic approach to data collection. For this, the researchers collect instances of a specific speech act as they encounter them in their daily lives. This has also been called the notebook or the diary method. Manes and Wolfson (1981: 115), for instance, used this method to investigate compliments in American English and they consider this to be 'the only reliable method' to collect data on any kind of speech act. Together with their students, the two authors collected 686 compliments that they encountered in a large range of everyday situations. The results indicated that the compliments collected in this way were surprisingly uniform. One specific pattern (NP {is/ looks} (really) ADJ) accounted for 53.6 per cent of all the compliments in their set. In this pattern, a noun phrase is followed by a copular verb (e.g., *is* or *looks*) and an adjectival subject complement consisting of an optional intensifier like *really* and a positive adjective. Examples are 'Your hair looks nice' or 'This is really good' (Manes and Wolfson 1981: 120). Together with two more formulae, this accounts for 85 per cent of all the compliments in the set. However, it seems possible that the 'almost total lack of originality' (1981: 115) may be a direct result of the data collection regime. The collectors might have been more likely to spot and record the more prototypical compliments and to miss unusual and indirect formulations.

A similar method was employed by Holmes (1988, 1990, 1995), who investigated compliments in New Zealand English. Her study was based on 484 compliment exchanges collected with the help of the ethnographic method. She focused her attention not only on the wording of the compliments but also on the gender patterns of the participants, their relationship towards each other and the topics of the compliments. She found that women give and receive significantly more compliments than men do and that most compliments received by women concern their appearance (Holmes 1988: 449, 455; 1995: 123, 132). However, Holmes also points out that the gender of the data collectors may have influenced some of these statistics as 92 per cent of them were female students (1988: 450).

2.6 Perception Studies

In more recent experimental work on speech acts, the research interest has moved from the different realisations of specific speech acts to the way that they are interpreted by listeners. Such studies generally provide prompts to the study participants and ask them to evaluate these prompts along certain dimensions. In some cases, the prompts are invented in order to manipulate specific aspects of the prompts. In other cases, real examples are used, for instance, from fictional sources such as movies or TV series. Such examples have the advantage that the speech act under investigation can be shown in its larger context and in its multimodal manifestation, including tone of voice, facial expressions, gestures and so on.

Murphy (2019: 225), for instance, used a series of sixteen invented apologies ranging from a real apology, 'I'm sorry I won't be able to come', to various sentences starting with 'I'm sorry' that are dubious cases of apologies or even clear cases of verbal formula mismatches in the sense of Culpeper (2011: 174). 'I'm sorry you won't be able to come', for instance, is perhaps an expression of sympathy rather than an apology and 'I'm sorry he is such an arsehole' is a verbal formula mismatch. In the experiment, recordings of the sixteen test phrases were played to the study participants, who were then asked to rate them for how apologetic they thought the speaker (always the same for all sixteen sentences) was, how bad the speaker felt and how they would feel after hearing this utterance on a six-point Likert scales (from 'not at all apologetic' to 'completely apologetic', from 'doesn't feel bad at all' to 'feels very bad' and from 'completely worse' to 'completely better'). The results show that people differ in what for them is an apology. Some participants even accepted verbal formula mismatches in which a clearly impolite comment is preceded by 'I'm sorry' as genuine apologies (Murphy 2019: 228).

Haugh and Chang (Chang and Haugh 2011; Haugh and Chang 2019), on the other hand, used one single intercultural telephone conversation involving apologetic behaviour to gauge the reactions of different study participants. In the recording, an Australian called Wayne apologises for not turning up to a dinner with the caller, a Taiwanese called Joyce, and her family. The situation is complex since there are several aspects in Wayne's behaviour that might have called for an apology. He and his wife did not turn up at the dinner in a Taiwanese restaurant, he failed to let Joyce and her family know in good time that they would not be turning up, and he did not return the call when Joyce tried to contact him from the restaurant. In the original study, Chang and Haugh (2011: 424) asked twenty-five English speaking Australians and twenty-five Chinese speaking Taiwanese to listen to a recording of the conversation and to evaluate it on a scale from polite to impolite and it turns out that the two groups show significant differences in how they evaluate this particular situation. The Taiwanese participants tended to evaluate the interaction towards the impolite end of the Likert scale, while many Australians opted for neutral or polite ratings. In the follow-up study, Haugh and Chang (2019) asked another fifty-five Australian respondents to evaluate the same recording and in their analysis focused more carefully on individual differences between the Australian speakers rather than the differences across the two linguacultures. Both studies highlight the variability of judgements of degrees of im/politeness and the importance of using highly contextualised speech acts in order to get nuanced and meaningful responses in experimental perception studies. The focus of such studies is on the variability of perception in a large number of study participants whilst the number of prompts is usually very small or, as in this case, just one.

2.7 Variation

The approaches to speech act studies reviewed in this section have in common that they generally focus on individual speech acts and that they employ empirical methods to do so. They also have in common that the researchers try to carefully control contrastive variables in order to compare the production (and reception) of speech acts across different types of speakers (and observers). Most of the approaches reviewed in the previous section use experimental methods to elicit their data and thus provide the potential of manipulating the relevant variables. This comes at the price of reduced authenticity. The researchers do not observe how people produce speech acts when they are not being observed. Instead, they observe various forms of how people think speech acts should be produced.

Some approaches reviewed try to reduce the artificiality of the experimental situation by creating more realistic scenarios or by focusing on naturally occurring contrastive contexts. But these approaches, too, focus on individual speech acts and their variability in relation to different types of speakers.

3 Corpus-Based Approaches

Corpus-based investigations of speech acts constitute the third wave of speech act studies. They abandon the careful experimental elicitation of speech acts and the construction or observation of comparable contexts and instead focus on the distribution and the range of actual manifestations of (possibly) large numbers of a given speech act in naturally occurring contexts. The researcher asks questions about the actual occurrences of speech acts and about the shapes they take in different contexts. The data is authentic because it is produced in actual communicative contexts which exist independently of the research project. Four different branches of corpus-based speech act studies are distinguished. Two branches search for the speech acts themselves (via typical expressions or typical patterns) while the other two branches search for meta-illocutionary expressions and use the retrieved hits to either provide a first order approach to how speakers talk about speech acts or to search for the named speech acts in the vicinity of the meta-illocutionary expression.

3.1 Identifying Speech Acts in Large Corpora

The first problem faced by corpus-based investigations is the identification of specific speech acts in whatever corpus is chosen for their investigation (for an overview see O'Keeffe 2018). Speech acts are functional entities, that is to say a compliment, for instance, is a compliment because it performs a certain communicative function and not because of a specific shape. Thus, the most obvious way of searching for specific speech acts in a large corpus would be for the researcher to read the entire text in a so-called manual search and pick out all the instances that can be found in the text. For large texts and entire corpora of texts with millions of words this is generally not feasible unless the researcher restricts the manual search to carefully chosen samples that are representative of the entire text or corpus (see Kohnen 2008 for a particularly careful outline of this methodology in a historical context). Computerised searches, however, depend on specific search strings and thus on recurring patterns that are known to occur in specific speech acts. In the following, I use the term 'corpus-based' in the narrow sense to refer to computerised searches of large corpora only (but see Section 6 for a combination of manual and computerised searches across large corpora).

Some speech acts often have relatively conventionalised shapes or they include elements like *sorry, please* or *hi*, that signal their function as an apology, a request or a greeting. Such elements are often known as illocutionary force indicating devices or IFIDs (Levinson 1983: 238). But as pointed out in Section 1, I prefer to follow Holmes (1984: 346), who proposed a distinction between the illocutionary point, that is to say the function or purpose of a speech act, and the illocutionary force, that is to say the strength with which a particular illocutionary point is communicated. According to this terminology, elements like *sorry, please* or *hi* will be called illocutionary point indicating devices (or IPIDs for short). Such elements may help in the detection of speech acts. Other speech acts are less predictable in their form, which makes it more difficult to retrieve them automatically. There are basically two solutions to this conundrum. One solution uses the typical patterns or IPIDs as search strings of the more conventionalised speech acts in spite of the problems of precision and recall that this involves.

The other solution uses the everyday descriptions of speech acts, the so-called meta-illocutionary lexicon (Schneider 2017, 2021, 2022), to retrieve passages in which people talk about speech acts. In some cases, the two solutions overlap, as for instance, in 'Let me apologize again for the delay' (COCA, FIC, 2018), in which the meta-illocutionary term *apologize* is used to actually perform an apology. Both solutions can be further subdivided into two different branches as shown in Figure 1. The search for specific speech act manifestations in a corpus can either use typical patterns as search strings or IPIDs. The search for meta-illocutionary expressions (MIEs) can be used in an investigation for the distribution and use of the meta-illocutionary expressions themselves or it can be used to manually search for occurrences of the named speech act in the close vicinity of the expression. These four types of investigation will be briefly introduced in the following two sections.

In some cases, corpora include pragmatic annotations that specify the speech-act function of utterances. The *SPICE-Ireland Corpus*, a subsection of the spoken component of the *ICE-Ireland Corpus* is a good example (see Landert et al. 2023: 15–16). With an annotated corpus, it should be easy to retrieve every

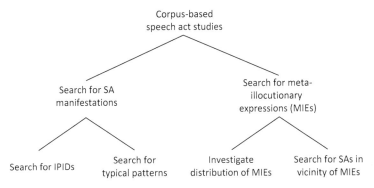

Figure 1 Four branches of corpus-based speech act studies

single instance of a specific speech act that is attested in this corpus, which would be the 'holy grail' of corpus pragmatics (O'Keeffe 2018: 599). However, there are some problems with this procedure. To apply pragmatic annotations to a corpus is extremely time-consuming and therefore pragmatically annotated corpora tend to be small. There have been attempts to carry out the annotation in a semi-automatic fashion (see, in particular, Weisser 2015, 2018), but annotations largely depend on clear and unambiguous labels that can be attached to relevant entities. As I will show in more detail in Section 4, speech acts are often enough fuzzy, ambivalent and even the result of discursive negotiations by the participants. This makes it difficult to provide an integral classification of all utterances of a corpus. Researchers who want to use an annotated corpus must ask themselves to what extent they are prepared to trust the categorisation provided by another researcher who may have had different research interests. In contrast to parts-of-speech taggers, which generally deal with formal elements of sentences, speech-act annotation deals with functional entities that are more difficult to classify. It is not impossible that current advances in the development of Large Language Models will soon lead to improved tools for automated pragmatic annotations. However, in the context of this Element, I will focus on the corpus-retrieval of individual utterances with specific speech-act values from un-annotated corpora.

3.2 Search for IPIDs

The early corpus-based speech act studies generally relied on illocutionary point indicating devices (IPIDs) to retrieve relevant speech acts. This meant that relatively conventionalised speech acts were preferred for such investigations. Relevant examples are requests, which often include *please*, apologies, which tend to include *sorry* or *pardon* or can even be performed by using such an IPID on its own, greetings, which can be performed by saying *hello* or *hi* or farewells that are often performed by *goodbye* or just *bye*. However, these elements are only typical but not obligatory for these speech acts. Requests can be performed without *please*, apologies without *sorry* and so on. Moreover, most of these elements can also occur in other contexts ('a sorry sight', 'he was sorry to hear about their accident', 'a present to please them'). It is, therefore, generally necessary to manually sort through all the hits returned by the computer and classify them as true or false.

Aijmer (1996) was one of the earliest researchers to use this method to investigate a range of conversational routines, as she called them, in the *London-Lund Corpus of Spoken English*, for example, thanking, apologies, requests and offers. In the chapter on thanking, for instance, Aijmer (1996: chapter 2) uses some 300 instances of thanking expressions retrieved from the corpus (*thank you, thank you so much, thanks, thanks very much indeed*, etc.) to find a range of regular patterns in the data, for example, in terms of thanks responses, their grammatical and prosodic realisation, their distribution across different text types as well as their functional profiles. Thanking expressions may be used as discourse markers, as closing signals, in proposal-acceptance sequences and so on.

Deutschmann (2003) used the same approach to investigate apologies in the spoken part of the *British National Corpus*. He identified a range of apology expressions (i.e., IPIDs) and with their help retrieved 3070 apologies. He claims that apologies are rarely produced without an apology expression. 'Apologising tends to be accompanied by a limited set of easily identifiable routine formulae. Of course, it is theoretically possible to apologise without saying *I'm sorry* or *excuse me* but research has shown that this is rarely the case in English' (Deutschmann 2003: 36). However, this claim is based on sources that used the diary method and discourse completion tasks to collect apologies and it is unclear whether the findings can be transferred to occurrences in large corpora (see Jucker 2018: 377 for details). However, the apologies that he was able to retrieve in this way allowed him to provide a range of interesting statistics about gender differences, age differences and social class differences of the apologisers, about the different types of offence leading to the apology, about the apparent sincerity levels of the apologies as well as about the variation in apologising across different conversational settings.

3.3 Search for Typical Patterns

In addition to IPIDs, some researchers have also tried to use conventionalised linguistic patterns as search strings in an attempt to retrieve specific speech acts from a corpus. Jucker et al. (2008), for instance, used a list of patterns that had been proposed by earlier research to retrieve compliments from the *British National Corpus*. As pointed out in Section 2.5, Manes and Wolfson had suggested that compliments in American English are remarkably lacking in originality. Three syntactic patterns accounted for 85 per cent of all the compliments in their collection (1981: 120–21). The formulae proposed by Manes and Wolfson required some modifications to make them practicable as search strings with reasonable precision and recall. Without these modifications, some strings retrieved far too many hits that were not compliments, so-called false positives. The first of Manes and Wolfson's formulae, for instance, consists of a noun phrase followed by a copular verb (e.g., *is* or *looks*) followed by an adjectival complement consisting of an optional intensifier and a positive adjective, as in 'Your hair looks nice' or 'This is very good'. However, there is no way to restrict the search string systematically to positive adjectives, which means that the search produces far too many hits, that is, it overgenerates and reduces precision. According to Manes and Wolfson, the intensifier is optional in this formula, but a search string without an intensifier also vastly overgenerates and makes it impracticable to manually exclude the false positives. If the intensifier is made an obligatory part of the search string, the retrieved set is more manageable but it undergenerates, because it misses strings such as 'Your hair looks nice' without an intensifier. The string, therefore, has a more limited recall. Similar adjustments were necessary for all the formulae proposed by Manes and Wolfson. However, the method allowed Jucker et al. (2008: 290) to retrieve 343 compliments that had all been manually verified.

The two methods, that is, the search for relevant IPIDs and the search for typical patterns, may be useful for speech acts that show a reasonably high degree of conventionalisation and speech acts that regularly include an IPID. But even in these cases, the methods are unlikely to retrieve all instances of a specific speech act from a corpus, and the researchers have no way of telling how much they are missing unless they manually inspect a representative part of the entire corpus, which in many cases may not be practicable. For less conventionalised speech acts, the methods become problematic. Speech acts that use unexpected patterns and do not use any of the IPIDs on the researcher's list are more difficult to be retrieved automatically if they can be retrieved at all. This is a particularly serious problem for researchers interested in the history of specific speech acts. Historical data may show a broader range of manifestations of specific speech acts and these manifestations may be less familiar from a present-day perspective. They require a manual approach. As a solution, Kohnen (2008) proposed the use of a carefully curated sample corpus for a manual search for relevant manifestations. They can then be used for searches in the entire corpus. I will come back to this problem in Section 6 on historical investigations.

3.4 Meta-Illocutionary Expressions

A second solution for the search of speech acts in a corpus does not search for a specific speech act itself but for passages in which this speech act is explicitly mentioned. This is part of the larger field of metapragmatics which investigates the ways in which people in their everyday discourse talk about the use of language (see Culpeper and Haugh 2014: chapter 8; Haugh 2018 for an overview). The expressions that they use for this purpose are called metapragmatic expressions. Haugh (2018: 624) distinguishes between expressions that refer to pragmatic acts and activities, such as *apologise, compliment, joke* or *tease*; expressions that refer to inferential acts and activities, such as *allude, hint, imply* or *insinuate*; and expressions that refer to evaluative acts and activities, such as *aggressive, considerate* or *polite*. Here, we are concerned with the first type only, that is, those expressions that refer to pragmatic acts and activities. Schneider (2017) proposed the term meta-illocutionary expressions for them and collectively they constitute the meta-illocutionary lexicon (see also Schneider 2021, 2022 and Schoppa 2022). In some cases, this terminology may be misleading if it includes speech act verbs that designate perlocutions rather than illocutions, such as *threaten* or *insult*, which cannot be used performatively (Schneider 2022).

The meta-illocutionary lexicon provides a first-order perspective on speech acts. It tells us how people talk about speech acts and it tells us which communicative acts are salient enough for the speakers of a language to give them a name and talk about them. Such a first-order perspective may well deviate from the second-order perspective taken by language philosophers in the deliberations about the felicity conditions of specific speech acts. Levinson (2015), too, has a different set of speech acts in mind when he talks about the undetermined and presumably undeterminable inventory of speech acts because he also includes speech acts without a vernacular name, such as continuers (*hmhm*), pre-closings (*well* at the end of phone calls), repair initiators (*excuse me?*) or pre-invitations (*What are you doing on Friday night?*) proposed by conversation analysts.

The meta-illocutionary lexicons of different languages can, therefore, be used as a tool in the analysis of culture-specific attitudes on human verbal communication. It has been argued, for instance, that commissive speech acts, that is, promising and other speech acts that commit the speaker to a future course of action, have a prominent position in Western societies while they play only a minor role in some non-Western societies (e.g., the Ilongots of the Philippines, cf. Verschueren 1994: 4138).

Meta-illocutionary expressions can perform various functions in everyday discourse. Schneider (2017: 230) distinguishes four functions: performative, reporting, problematising and challenging, while Schoppa (2022: 71) extends this classification and distinguishes six functions: performative, problematising, reporting, clarifying, naming and commenting. Extracts 3.1 to 3.3 illustrate the performative, the problematising and the reporting functions, respectively. They have been retrieved from the *Corpus of Contemporary American English* (COCA).

3.1 I compliment you on that very difficult reporting work. (COCA, SPOK, 2014)

3.2 You seem the more motherly of the two of you. (. . .) I think he's meaning it as a compliment. Well, it doesn't sound like a compliment. (COCA, MOV, 2019)

3.3 'Thank you. I admire your tenacity.' He acknowledged the compliment. (COCA, FIC, 2015)

In 3.1, the speaker uses the meta-illocutionary expression *compliment* to actually perform a compliment. In 3.2, the two speakers debate the status of a previous utterance for which it is not clear whether it was meant as a compliment or not and in 3.3, the narrator merely reports that the recipient of a compliment acknowledged it.

In addition to the distinction of different functions of meta-illocutionary expressions, Schneider (2017, 2021, 2022) and Schoppa (2022) are mainly interested in the occurrences and distribution of these expressions. Schneider (2022), for instance, investigates the occurrence of meta-illocutionary expressions in Irish English. He provides statistics that show their distribution across speech and writing and finds that one of these expressions, *apology* and its derived word forms are more frequent in spoken language than in written language. He also provides statistics for *apology* and its derived word forms across different text categories, but the two corpora used for this purpose, ICE-Ireland and SPICE-Ireland, are relatively small and the attested numbers of occurrences are too small for reliable generalisations. Schoppa (2022) asked similar questions and investigated *request* and *apology* and their derived word forms in the BNC and in the COCA. He shows that the differences across British and American English are relatively small, but there are clear differences between the two illocutions under investigation. It turns out, for instance, that in British English the performative function of meta-illocutionary expressions denoting apologies is more frequent than in American English while the commenting function and the reporting function shows higher frequencies in American English than in British English. Thus, British speakers use these expressions more often to perform apologies while American speakers use them more often to talk about them.

3.5 MIEs as a Link to Actual Speech Acts

Meta-illocutionary expressions are also interesting in corpus-based speech act investigations because they may lead the researchers to actual manifestations of the speech act in question. If the meta-illocutionary expression is used performatively, it is actually part of the speech act itself and the search for the expression will immediately reveal one specific manifestation of the speech act as in Extract 3.1 above. If the meta-illocutionary expression is used in a non-performative function, for example, reporting or problematising, the actual speech act talked about may be found in close vicinity of the metapragmatic expression, as in Extracts 3.2 and 3.3 above. In either case, the method requires a painstaking, manual analysis of all the retrieved hits, or at least of representative and sufficiently large samples of all retrieved hits. This may allow a variety of research questions to be explored across different parts of a corpus, different text genres or possibly even across different speaker demographics if the relevant information has been coded into the corpus under investigation.

The speech act manifestations retrieved with this method provide an interesting first-order perspective into the manifestations that the speakers themselves consider to be either clear or disputable cases of a certain speech act. The set is likely to include not only prototypical manifestations but also less expected ones. At the same time, it is likely that the retrieved set is somewhat biased as unusual formulations of a specific speech act may be more likely to provoke some discussion about them.

Jucker and Taavitsainen (2014) used this method to trace compliments in the history of American English. They searched for the meta-illocutionary expression *compliment* in five samples drawn at even intervals from the two centuries covered by the *Corpus of Historical American English* (COHA) and the *Corpus of Contemporary American English* (COCA) to retrieve 1741 passages in which the expression occurred. Two trained coders inspected these passages manually and tried to locate the speech act referred to and to code each instance according to several dimensions, that is, the type of compliment (personal or ceremonious), the gender of the complimenter and the recipient of the compliment, the object of the compliment and the compliment response. Not all retrieved passages contained enough information to code for every of these dimensions, but the number of codable compliments was high enough to reveal some interesting developments over the two centuries covered by the two corpora. It turned out, for instance, that between 70 and 85 per cent of all compliments in all periods were given by men in contrast to previous research (carried out with different research methods, see Section 2.5) that had reported that compliments are more often paid and received by women (Holmes 1988, 1990, 1995). And it also turned out that across the two centuries, the recipients of compliments became more and more likely to accept the compliment.

Jucker (2018) used the same methodology to trace the forms and functions of apologies in the fiction section of the *Corpus of Historical American English*. Here, the search term *apolog** was used to retrieve passages containing the meta-illocutionary expression *apology* or one of its derivative word forms in each of four subsamples of the corpus containing the material for five decades. The results showed that the number of analysable apologies retrieved in this way increased very considerably from the first to the last half-centuries and it showed some interesting developments of the strategies used to perform an apology. The use of an apology expression, such as *sorry, excuse* or *apologise* (here called illocutionary point indicating devices) increased over time while taking responsibility for the offence by the speaker and providing an explanation or account why the offence happened decreased.

Such studies provide interesting new insights into specific speech acts and how they developed over time, but the method clearly has some limitations. It only retrieves passages in which speakers feel a need to explicitly talk about a speech act. As pointed out above, this might well privilege less typical formats. Moreover, the method is labour intensive. It requires dedicated coders who analyse large numbers of retrieved hits and elaborate testing to determine the reliability of the categories and a consistent coding by the coders. I will return to corpus-based approaches in the context of Section 6 on historical speech act studies, in which they are the default method because experimental approaches are impossible for obvious reasons.

In the next section, I turn to speech act studies that I have labelled fourth-wave approaches (see Section 1). They are less interested in the variability of speech acts across different groups of speakers and recipients but more in the local contexts in which individual specimens occur, how they are discursively negotiated by the participants and how they are often a mutual achievement rather than an individual product by one speaker only.

4 'Is That Supposed to Be an Insult or a Compliment?': Discursive Approaches

Recently, speech acts have increasingly been seen as fuzzy entities. Their nature (illocutionary point) cannot be established simply on the basis of felicity conditions (as was assumed by the early language philosophers). The illocutionary potential of utterances is often negotiated by conversationalists. This requires a shift in research methods. The analysis needs to focus on sequences of utterances and on the negotiation between the interactants. A specific utterance may receive its illocutionary potential in and through the reaction it provokes from the interlocutor. This section introduces two scales that are important for the fuzziness of speech acts: the cline of illocutionary indeterminacy and the cline of illocutionary force. The final part in this section will then argue why the fuzziness along these two scales is not a weakness or even a problem for our communication but in fact an essential asset.

4.1 A Discursive Perspective

Scott and Cath, two characters in the novel *We Are Still Tornadoes* by Michael Kun and Susan Mullen, exchange letters after graduating from high school. Cath has gone off to college while Scott has started to work at his father's men's clothing shop in their hometown. In one of her early letters, Cath, in an exchange of playful banter, suggests that she is going to call Scott 'underachiever guy' if he keeps calling her 'college girl'. In his next letter, Scott asks, 'Calling me "underachiever guy" – is that supposed to be an insult or a compliment?' (Kun and Mullen 2016: 17–18). It appears that the illocutionary point of using this particular designation for him is unclear, or at least can be argued by Scott not to be clear. It can be taken as an insult or as a compliment. In her next letter, Cath disambiguates her speech act. 'And the "underachiever guy" thing is a compliment, as far as you know. It means you're super smart, but you don't apply yourself' (p. 19). On this reading, the speech act is ambiguous for Scott, the addressee, but not for Cath, who, in her response, assigns it a very specific illocutionary point. Scott is not convinced, though. In a postscript to his next letter, he muses, '"Underachiever guy" was an insult, wasn't it. Damn!' (p. 28). But in her next letter, Cath also adds a postscript and modifies her initial illocutionary point assignment. 'P.P.S. "Underachiever guy" isn't an insult. But I guess it's not exactly a compliment, either. It's a combination of the two. It's an "insultiment"' (p. 31).

It appears that the illocutionary point of an utterance can be disputed by the interactants. The felicity conditions à la Searle are not sufficient to disambiguate the utterance. In Section 4.2 following, I am going to describe this as a case of illocutionary indeterminacy. While some utterances encode their illocutionary point in a seemingly clear and unambiguous way, other utterances are indeterminate – and, as I shall argue, often deliberately so – about their illocutionary point.

Rieger (2017) discusses a similar case of two fictional characters who negotiate the illocutionary point of an utterance. It occurs in a brief episode from the sitcom series *The Big Bang Theory*, in which Sheldon has to apologise to his girlfriend Amy. Sheldon, a theoretical physicist at Caltech, has been forced to take a vacation but instead decides to help Amy, a neuroscientist, in her research lab as he does not really know how to take a proper vacation. The first day ends in a minor disaster because he is unhappy with the menial tasks that he is first given and then fails with a more delicate task. He breaks some equipment, cuts himself and faints at the sight of his own blood. The next day, he somewhat remorsefully returns to the lab to continue his holiday job, but Amy expects an apology first. Sheldon's explanation, 'I was not myself, I had lost a lot of thumb blood' is dismissed by Amy: 'that's not an apology'. She insists, 'I want a real apology' (see Extract 4.1).

4.1　*The Big Bang Theory* (Season 5, Episode 16) (Rieger 2017: 568; simplified)
1　Amy: I want a real apology
2　Sheldon: I'm sorry that you weren't able to–
3　Amy: no
4　Sheldon: that my genius
5　Amy: no
6　Sheldon: that the soap was
7　Amy: SHELdon
8　Sheldon: fine
9　Amy: ((turns to look at Sheldon))
10　Sheldon: sorry
11　Amy: you're forgiven. Now if you wanna stay, get started on these beakers. They're still dirty from yesterday

Rieger points out how the opening of the scene creates an expectation of some offence-remedial-related action from Sheldon for what has happened on the previous day. But Sheldon, who she describes as 'highly intelligent, "geeky nerd" who [has] difficulties with interpersonal relationships' and 'is lacking social skills' (Rieger 2017: 566), tries to explain rather than apologise. Amy rejects his various attempts as unsatisfactory and disqualifies them as inappropriate, until he actually manages to say an unmitigated 'sorry' without blaming Amy or the situation for what happened on the previous day.

In this case, the discussion focuses not only on the nature of the speech act, its illocutionary point, but also on its level of sincerity, its illocutionary force. Is it really meant as a sincere apology with the required level of regret for what has happened? In Section 4.3 I will discuss such cases in terms of their illocutionary force.

In the two fictional cases briefly discussed above, characters discursively negotiate the value of specific speech acts. The characters talk on a meta level about their own utterances and what they mean. They evaluate each other's and their own utterances, and they negotiate these evaluations. This is, then, a discursive approach because it focuses on the discourse of the interactants themselves and it focuses on the problematising function of the meta-illocutionary lexicon introduced in the previous section (Section 3.5). What is at issue is no longer the academic definitions proposed by philosophers or pragmaticists on the basis of felicity conditions (i.e., second-order definitions), but on the expressions used in everyday discourse to refer to specific utterances and their communicative functions (i.e., first-order definitions). The inventory of speech acts now encompasses those and only those communicative acts that are salient enough for language users to explicitly talk about them.

4.2 The Clines of Illocutionary Indeterminacy

Once we have made the move away from considering individual speech acts and their defining features in order to look at how conversationalists label and negotiate utterances, both their own and their interlocutor's, we see that the illocutionary potential of an utterance is, or rather can be, fuzzy in multiple ways (see also Jucker in press, where I develop similar ideas in a slightly different context). Figure 2 represents this in the form of a cline from clear-cut cases on the left to indeterminate ones on the right with a few examples of what are possibly compliments. The examples on the left look like prototypical compliments because they express praise about the addressee in an explicit and rather conventionalised way. They may even include an explicit performative, that is, a verb that spells out the illocutionary point of the utterance ('Let me compliment you'). In both cases, it is, of course, possible that the speaker uses the utterance ironically. This has to be assessed on the basis of the addressee's reaction. The explicit encoding of the illocutionary point can be deceptive.

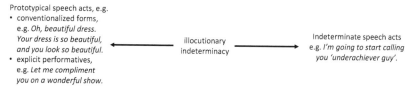

Figure 2 Cline of illocutionary indeterminacy (Examples from COCA)

What counts in a discursive approach is the way in which the interlocutors jointly negotiate the illocutionary point of an utterance. This can be done implicitly through the addressee's reaction to the compliment or explicitly by switching to a meta level and talk about the intended status of the utterance.

Strubel-Burgdorf (2018: 31) has a somewhat similar scale in mind when she places compliments and positive assessments on a continuum. For the examples that she retrieved from the *Santa Barbara Corpus of Spoken American English* (SBCSAE) it is often difficult to decide whether they are heard as one or the other. The more impersonal formulations, such as 'This was a really great meal' are more likely to be understood as a positive assessment whilst formulations including the speaker and positive assessments of the hearer are more likely to come across as compliments (2018: 32).

Most research on speech acts has traditionally focused on the cases on the far left of the cline in Figure 2. They include cases in which the illocutionary point is clearly indicated by a word or a phrase that is typical for this particular speech act, elements that have traditionally been called illocutionary force indicating devices or IFIDs (Levinson 1983: 238) but which I prefer to call illocutionary point indicating devices or IPIDs (following Holmes 1984: 346, see chapter 1). The connection between such IPIDs and specific speech acts is so strong, that IPIDs have regularly been used in corpus studies to retrieve these speech acts, for instance by Aijmer (1996) and Deutschmann (2003) (see Section 3). And Jucker et al. (2008) used a small number of syntactic patterns proposed by Manes and Wolfson (1981) to retrieve compliments from the BNC. In all these cases, only more or less prototypical manifestations of specific speech acts are retrieved and it is uncertain how many instances located further to the right of the cline of illocutionary indeterminacy are missed. These studies are based on the premise that utterances can generally be assigned to a specific speech act category.

The fictional examples discussed at the beginning of this section suggest that this is not always the case. The illocutionary point of an utterance can also be left open. The *Corpus of Contemporary American English* (COCA) provides a large range of examples in which interlocutors discuss the illocutionary point of specific utterances, see Extracts 4.2 to 4.12. These extracts were retrieved by performing some random collocation searches, for example, a search for the expressions *compliment* in close vicinity (within four words to the left or right) of the expression *insult* and so on.

4.2   I didn't know if that was a compliment or an insult. (COCA, FIC, 2017)

4.3   I texted back that I wasn't sure whether he'd meant it as a compliment or a gentle insult. (COCA, WEB, 2012)

4.4   I don't know if that's a compliment or an insult. (COCA, SPOK, 2015)

4.5   but then I was not sure whether 'small' would be a compliment or an insult. (COCA, FIC, 2011)

4.6   Is that a request or a command, Doctor? (COCA, TV, 2018)

4.7   It wasn't a question or a request, but a command. (COCA, WEB, 2012)

4.8   You cannot command me! – I do not command. I request. (COCA, FIC, 2003)

4.9   That's a warning, not a threat. (COCA, BLOG, 2012)

4.10   'She Remembers Everything' can be taken, I think, maybe as a promise or a threat. (COCA, SPOK, 2018)

4.11   Now, this is not a warning or a threat. I am just telling you. (COCA, TV, 2009)

4.12   She knows the way it sounded like a threat and not a warning. (COCA, FIC, 2004)

These random examples, which could easily be multiplied, show how the illocutionary point of an utterance is regularly under discussion. People are uncertain whether it is one or the other or whether it is a bit of both at the same time. In some cases, one of the interlocutors resolves any uncertainty and specifies a specific value to whatever utterance may have been unclear. In other cases, the uncertainty appears to remain. It is an open question as to how pervasive such discursive negotiations are and how often fuzzy or ambiguous utterances are accepted as sufficiently clear for current purposes by the interlocutors. Extracts 4.2 to 4.12 were retrieved from different sections of the *Corpus of Contemporary American English*. They come from fictional sources (FIC and TV) as well as from texts posted on the Internet (WEB and BLOG) and from conversational data (SPOK).

4.3 The Cline of Illocutionary Force

Rieger's (2017) example from *The Big Bang Theory* quoted at the beginning of this section demonstrates a different cline. As pointed out above, the situational context of Sheldon turning up in Amy's lab makes an apology highly expectable and whatever utterance Sheldon produces is being assessed by Amy as being a sufficient or an insufficient apology. What seems to be at issue here and what is negotiated explicitly by Amy and Sheldon is the illocutionary force of the utterance, that is, the strength or sincerity with which the apology comes across. Sheldon may well be aware of what is expected from him, but he prefers to give some weak excuses rather than an unambiguous apology while Amy rejects all his attempts until he actually produces an unmitigated *sorry*, which she then immediately accepts by moving on in the conversation and by assigning him some new tasks.

Figure 3 Cline of illocutionary force (Examples from COCA)

In Figure 2, we have seen that speech acts are often negotiated in terms of their illocutionary point. For apologies it appears to be particularly relevant to assess not only their point (Is it an apology or not?) but also their force (Is it a deep and heartfelt apology or a casual and perfunctory one?) (see Figure 3).

On the far left of the scale, there are apologies that are explicit and come across as heartfelt. The speaker takes extra care to upgrade the apology in order to convince the addressee that the apology is sincere by using intensifiers (*really, terribly*) and more elaborate and less conventional constructions. On the far right of the scale there are apologies that appear to be casual and perfunctory. They are typically short and conventionalised. In some cases, they may be mere spill cries (such as *oops* or *whoops*) with an uncertain apologetic status.

Extracts 4.13 to 4.24 provide some random examples taken from the *Corpus of Contemporary American English*. There is no claim that these examples have very precise positions on the cline of illocutionary force, but they illustrate the fact that apologies can differ significantly along this cline.

4.13   We beg your most humble pardon (COCA, FIC, 2003)

4.14   I most humbly apologize (COCA, MOV, 2001)

4.15   Oh, I'm really terribly sorry. (COCA, MOV, 1994)

4.16   Sorry I took so long. (COCA, SPOK, 2012)

4.17   Yeah, sorry, go ahead. (COCA, MOV, 2010)

4.18   Sorry, we're all full. (COCA, TV, 1998)

4.19   Oops. Sorry about that. (COCA, MOV, 2006)

4.20   didn't know that; oops! (COCA, GLOG, 2012)

4.21   'Have you taken your medication today?' 'Whoops', she said, grinning. (COCA, FIC, 2006)

4.22   Oops, I forgot (COCA, SPOK, 1999)

4.23   soz, brad (COCA, WEB, 2012)

4.24   Marv gave Vanessa an apologetic shrug (COCA, FIC, 2010)

It is, of course, possible that some of these apologies are highly ironic and only pretend to be sincere and heartfelt. Intuitively this appears to be a likely scenario for the more elaborate apologies higher up on the scale. The speaker and the addressee will both have their own assessments of the adequacy of the chosen formulation, and, if necessary, they will discursively negotiate this value, as in the case of Amy in Extract 4.1, who insisted over several turns to get a 'real apology'. Extracts 4.13, 4.14 and 4.15 illustrate speakers that appear to take great care to produce a sincere sounding apology by adding intensifiers and by using somewhat elaborate constructions. In extracts 4.16, 4.17 and 4.18 the formulations are more conventionalised. The utterances are clearly recognisable as apologies, but they do not have the same force and the same appearance of sincerity as the previous ones. In extract 4.19, the IPID *sorry* is accompanied by a spill cry, *oops*, which seems to reduce the sincerity of the apology. The speaker seems to suggest that what happened was merely a trivial mishap rather than a real offence requiring a real apology. Extracts 4.20, 4.21 and 4.22 are less clear cases of apologies. The speaker merely utters a spill cry to express some dismay or surprise about a minor mishap. Extract 4.23 uses *soz*, a short form of *sorry* that seems to have spread in social media channels in recent years and is usually used in non-serious contexts. Extract 4.24, finally, is an example in which a narrator describes a nonverbal apology. A fictional character gives an apologetic shrug. This example is particularly interesting because here the apology is maximally vague for the addressee(s), that is, some other fictional character(s), but the illocutionary point is explicitly communicated by the narrator to the implied reader of this text. Narrative texts often provide descriptions of the non-verbal aspects of specific communicative acts. For the readers, the communicative intention is made explicit, but it is unclear to what extent an apologetic shrug or smile is recognised by the fictional addressee or to what extent it would be recognised by a non-fictional addressee. I will come back to such examples in Section 5.

Holmes (1984) provides an interesting categorisation of different elements that can be used to increase (boost) or decrease (attenuate) the illocutionary force of specific speech acts. Thus, 4.25, said by one close friend to another, can be boosted as in 4.26 or attenuated as in 4.27 by appropriate modifiers (Holmes 1984: 347, italics original).

4.25   You are pretty.

4.26   *Really* you are *amazingly* pretty.

4.27   You are *kind of* pretty *in a way*.

Depending on the type of speech act, boosting or attenuating may have different effects. While the attenuation in 4.27 reduces the force of the compliment and thus, perhaps, makes it less positive for the addressee, an attenuated criticism may have the oppositive effect of making the criticism less negative for the addressee, as in 4.28 (Holmes 1984: 346, italics original).

4.28   You are *a bit of* a fool *you know*.

Thus, the boosters or attenuators change the affective meaning of a speech act in ways that depend on the default function of the speech act. Similar boosters or attenuators can be used for other speech act types as well, for example, in promises, such as 4.29 and 4.30, said by a husband to his wife (Holmes 1984: 437).

4.29   *I solemnly promise* I won't be late home today.

4.30   *I guess* I'll *probably* ring you later.

Holmes developed these insights in the context of a first-wave approach on the basis of invented examples, but they show how the force of speech acts can be systematically varied along the cline that I have presented in Figure 3 (see also Schegloff 2007: 83 and Haugh 2015: 247 for ways of attenuating the force of utterances).

The examples discussed above show that speakers regularly modify the force of specific speech acts and again, extracts can easily be found in the *Corpurs of Contemporary American English* in which interlocutors discursively negotiate the force of their utterances, as in Extracts 4.31 to 4.35.

4.31   Why don't you just do the right thing and give a real apology? (COCA, SPOK, 2005)

4.32   That is not a real apology. You did not mean that at all. (COCA, TV, 2011)

4.33   They apologized. I felt the apology was sincere. (COCA, SPOK, 2015)

4.34   'It wasn't a real promise', she protested. (COCA, FIC, 2013)

4.35   Tom do you really mean that? Is your promise sincere? (COCA, WEB, 2012)

As in the case of negotiations of the illocutionary point of an utterance discussed above, it would be interesting to find out how frequent such first-order discussions of illocutionary force are in the data and whether there are significant differences between different registers, but at present this is a question that awaits empirical investigation.

Previous research has shown that the cline of illocutionary force also has a diachronic relevance (see Jucker 2019). Early forms of apologies as attested in the available corpora invariably showed an elaborate format with little or no conventionalisation. In fact, the earliest apologies in Old English appear to have taken the form of religious confessions of sins perpetrated against God. Later attestations included confessions/sincere apologies to a fellow human being until the repertoire of apologies was extended to also include increasingly conventionalised and less weighty apologies. Today, as the examples 4.13 to 4.24 have shown, speakers have a very broad range of formats, from the creative and sincere to the conventionalised and perfunctory, at their disposal to match them carefully to the current communicative needs (see Section 6 for more details on the diachronic development of some selected speech acts).

4.4 The Relevance of Indeterminacy

As we have seen, interlocutors often discursively negotiate the illocutionary point and the illocutionary force of a particular utterance. They retrospectively question what has just been produced by somebody else or they prospectively try to elicit a specific speech act from their interlocutor. However, in most cases, such discursive negotiations do not seem to be necessary. The conversation runs smoothly back and forth and there appears to be (a tacit) agreement between the interlocutors as to the pragmatic acts they are engaged in. It is these seemingly unproblematic cases that have been the focus of attention of speech act research throughout the first three waves of speech act theory (see Section 1 for details). In principle, every utterance was considered to have a specific and well-defined illocutionary point. Disputes between interlocutors about the illocutionary point of an utterance were largely ignored or considered to be special cases without any impact on the outlines of a theory speech acts.

A discursive approach to speech acts takes a somewhat different perspective. It views speech acts as negotiable entities. A conversation that runs smoothly does not necessarily imply that the interlocutors always agree on the specific illocutionary points of their utterances. It merely indicates that the understanding is sufficiently good for current purposes. In some cases, the illocutionary point and the illocutionary force may be explicitly encoded leaving little room for doubt ('I most humbly apologise'). In other cases, the illocutionary point and force are less clear but sufficiently clear for current purposes. They may even be maximally vague ('I was not myself' said as an apology) without creating any problems in the interaction. Alternatively, if a speaker misjudges the necessary level of specificity or if the interlocutors disagree about what is appropriate at a given point in the conversation, there might be a need for remedial or at least discursive action.

Jucker, Smith and Lüdge (2003) used a Relevance Theoretic framework to argue that vague utterances can be more relevant and thus communicatively more efficient than more precise ones because they require less processing effort in cases where a more precise formulation would not provide any additional information. In their data, a speaker told a person he did not know very well about some travelling and mentioned that he 'passed by a place where I lived for a while' (Jucker, Smith and Lüdge 2003: 1745). It is clear that the speaker could have provided a more precise description of this place, but for the current purposes of telling a relative stranger a vague designation seemed to be good enough because it did not involve any unnecessary processing effort. In the speaker's estimation, the place name would not have yielded any additional contextual effects.

In the same way, utterances may communicate their illocutionary point clearly and explicitly or rather vaguely and ambiguously. Speakers may prefer to choose a vague formulation because they think that a more explicit formulation would not yield any additional useful information, because they do not want to commit themselves to a higher degree, or because they want to retain a degree of deniability. The speaker encodes as much information about the illocutionary point and the illocutionary force as seems warranted by the current situation. Under normal circumstances, this is entirely unproblematic and the conversation can continue to run smoothly. However, there may also be some disagreement between the speaker and the addressee as to how much explicitness is needed. Or the addressee may disagree with what he or she assumed was the speaker's chosen illocutionary point. In these cases, a discursive argument may be started to talk at a meta level about the illocutionary point and the illocutionary force of some utterance. This leads to cases that were illustrated in the opening part of this section.

5 'He Gave an Apologetic Shrug': Speech Acts and Multimodality

Narrative accounts of interactions often describe speech acts together with a specific gesture or facial expression of the speaker. In some cases, gestures alone appear to have an illocutionary potential (the narrator talks of a grateful smile or an apologetic shrug, for instance). In this section, I explore the potential of a multimodal perspective on speech acts and discuss its impact on speech act theory. In particular, silent 'speech acts', that is, mere gestures or facial expressions with an illocutionary potential, pose a considerable challenge to traditional speech act theory. They are further evidence of the fuzzy and negotiable nature of speech acts. In certain situations, speakers are clearly reluctant to commit themselves to an explicit illocution. An apologetic shrug may carry much less self-blame than an explicit 'I am sorry for what I have done'.

5.1 The Multimodality of Conversations

When we talk to each other in face-to-face interactions, we communicate not only through the words that we use. We also communicate through the way we position our bodies to our interlocutors, through gestures that we use while talking, through our facial expressions and through our voice quality, the loudness of our voice and so on. Communication is multimodal, but so far linguistics in general and speech act theory in particular has had surprisingly little to say on these aspects of communication and instead focuses almost entirely on the actual words used in the exchange. Holmes (1984: 350) is typical in this respect: 'Gesture, body posture, facial expression, hesitations, pauses and tone of voice are obvious examples of kinesic and paralinguistic devices which may modify illocutionary force. I have focussed, however, only on linguistic devices'. She is not alone in this even forty years later. To some extent this is understandable given the complexity of the task to disentangle the various contributions provided by gestures, facial expression and voice quality on the way we interpret what somebody says. It is not easy to distinguish in a principled way whether a gesture, for instance, has been made with a communicative intention or whether it was just an accidental hand or body movement or indeed a movement made with some non-communicative intention, to move into a more comfortable position or to reach for a glass of water.

In contrast to verbal communication, non-verbal aspects of communication show very little conventionalisation if any at all. It is difficult to identify discrete units and it is difficult to distinguish between communicative and non-communicative elements, which means that linguistics or pragmatics do not have the necessary analytical tools for their investigation. Such tools have been and are being developed, for instance, in the area of gesture studies (see Kendon 2004, 2017; McNeill 2005, 2012, 2015; Müller et al. 2013; Müller et al. 2014).

In this section, I cannot do justice to the rich literature on gestures and other forms of non-verbal communication. Instead, I propose an exploratory investigation of what the speakers, or rather writers, consider to be important multimodal aspects of communication and in particular how they describe gestures and facial expressions that are used to accompany or to replace speech acts. Such descriptions regularly occur in narrative fiction, in which a narrator describes the communicative behaviour of characters who interact with each other. Extracts 5.1 to 5.6 provide some relevant examples taken from the fiction section of the *Corpus of Contemporary American English*.

5.1 He gave me an apologetic smile and leaned back in his seat, silent as the late King Tut.

5.2 Lily glanced at Jenny, questioning, but the mercenary merely shrugged.

5.3 He waved goodbye and sailed across the lake.

5.4 Mrs. Flannery smiled apologetically. 'I'm sorry', she whispered.

5.5 Smedley Faversham nodded approvingly. 'I've always been in favor', he said.

5.6 'Thank you', she said, smiling at him gratefully.

In these examples, the narrator describes facial expressions and gestures, such as smiling, glancing, waving and nodding, in connection with the pragmatic acts of apologising, asking, leave taking, approving and thanking. In the first three cases, the pragmatic act appears to consist of a facial expression or a gesture only, while in the remaining three cases, the gesture is accompanied by speech.

It is an open question to what extent the fictional characters in each of these extracts recognised the illocutionary point of the facial expression or gesture, but the reader is provided with an explicit link between the gesture and the pragmatic act. I will return to this question in Section 5.3. Such passages appear to be rare outside of narrative contexts. For this reason, the current section focuses mostly on data taken from the fiction section of the *Corpus of Contemporary American English*.

I again adopt a first-order perspective and analyse what is sufficiently salient for language users to make it a topic of their conversation, or rather their narratives, even if this ignores some of the more nuanced distinctions that gesture specialists might be able to discern when they observe and analyse everyday conversations. Nevertheless, it may be useful to introduce a few basic distinctions proposed within the literature on gesture studies as a starting point for these explorations.

5.2 How to Communicate with Gestures

According to Kendon (2004: 7) gestures are visible actions that are part of what for others counts 'as an attempt by the actor to "give" information of some sort'. He reserves the term for actions and movements that are at least to some extent under the actor's voluntary control. Inadvertent actions and movements that people make, for instance, when they are nervous, such as adjustments of the hair or clothing, self-grooming or repetitive manipulation of items, such as rings or necklaces, are excluded. Such inadvertent actions may well be communicative in the overall impression that they provide for other people, but they are not part of gesture studies. '"Gesture" we suggest, then, is a label for actions that have the features of manifest deliberate expressiveness. They (. . .) tend to be directly perceived as being under the guidance of the observed person's voluntary control and being done for the purposes of expression rather than in the service of some practical aim' (Kendon 2004: 15).

For the analytical work in the area of gesture studies the distinction between gestures and other visible actions is important, and therefore requires a precise definition. The current section, however, adopts a first-order perspective and focuses on those visible bodily actions that people find sufficiently salient to talk about them. Kendon (2004: 8) excludes laughter, smiling and weeping from his definition of gestures, unless they were 'put on' as a show or performance rather than as a genuine expression of emotion. For narrators in the fictional texts that provide the bulk of the examples in this section the distinction does not appear to be important. As I will show in the following section, smiling is by far the most frequent visible action that is mentioned in connection with specific

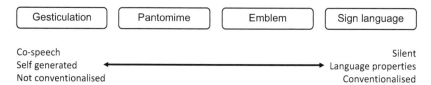

Figure 4 Gesture continuum (based on McNeill 2012: 5)

pragmatic acts and in most cases there is little to suggest that the smiling was only 'put on' without any genuine expression of emotion.

Gestures can be placed on a continuum represented in Figure 4, which is based on McNeill (2012: 5) and somewhat simplified. This continuum is based on three dimensions. Moving from left to right, the obligatory presence of speech decreases, the language-like properties increase and the gestures become more conventionalised.

Gesticulation on the far left of the continuum is usually part of the process of speaking. According to McNeill (2012: 4), 90 per cent of descriptive speech is accompanied by gesticulation. It is spontaneously generated by the speaker and not conventionalised. A pantomime is a simulation of an action or an object without speech. It is not coded and if there is speech it is not necessarily coordinated with the performance. McNeill (2012: 7) provides the example of a pantomime depicting somebody taking a key out of their pocket and opening a door, which may or may not be accompanied by an utterance, such as, 'There is only one thing to do'. Emblems are more conventionalised. They tend to have relatively fixed meanings that can be listed and reported, as the 'OK' sign or the offensive 'finger' sign. The thumbs-up and thumbs-down signs with reported origins in ancient Rome have even become some of the most widely used emoticons. Sign languages, finally, have all the properties of oral languages, except that they are silent. They are languages in their own right. Their signs are highly conventionalised and combine into larger constructions.

The gestures that speakers describe in connection with pragmatic acts are not easy to locate on this continuum. As the Extracts 5.1 to 5.6 have shown, the gestures may accompany verbal utterances or they may form a silent pragmatic act on their own. The degree of conventionalisation is debatable in many cases. In fact, the results presented in the next section show that some gestures very regularly appear in the context of specific pragmatic acts, either accompanying a verbal utterance or performing the pragmatic act silently. Nodding, for instance, regularly occurs in the context of agreeing, greeting, approving and replying. Smiling often occurs in the context of greeting, replying and apologising. And waving often occurs in the context of greeting and dismissing. In such contexts, the gestures may be closer to the status of an emblem than gesticulation. The fact that they are explicitly mentioned by the narrator more-over indicates that they all share the feature of reportability which McNeill ascribes to emblems but not to gesticulation.

5.3 Apologetic Gestures in Fiction

Fictional texts turn out to be particularly interesting for an investigation of multimodal pragmatic acts because there are often narrators who not only report what characters say to each other but who also explicitly assign illocutionary points to utterances and even to silent gestures. Jucker (2023) developed a method to investigate the multimodality of apologies and their politeness potential in fictional texts. He used collocation searches with the adjective *apologetic* and the adverb *apologetically* in the *Corpus of Contemporary American English* (COCA). The tool for retrieving relevant collocates does not allow a restriction to a specific section, but it turned out that most of the hits were found in the fiction section of COCA (see Jucker 2023: 336 for details). The results for each word form consisted in lists of nouns, verbs, adjectives and adverbs that regularly co-occur with each of these word forms. The lists were then manually searched for terms that denote gestures and co-occur at least three times with the relevant search term. In this way, ten gesture expressions were retrieved for the adjective *apologetic*: *smile* n., *look* n., *glance* n., *shrug* n., *smile* v., *gesture* n., *wave* n., *shrug* v., *grimace* n. and *nod* n. And eight expressions were retrieved for the adverb *apologetically*: *smile* v., *shrug* v., *glance* v., *shake* v., *nod* v., *grin* v., *wave* v. and *gesture* v. The two lists overlap to a great extent and indicate the range of visible bodily actions that are regularly associated with the pragmatic act of apologising. Some items need a brief explanation. The noun *wave* is ambiguous between a hand gesture and curling water, but an inspection of all cases showed that it is only the hand gesture that collocates with *apologetic*. The verb *shake* in itself does not describe a gesture, but in all relevant cases, *shake* was used in combination with *head*.

The most frequent gesture expression collocating with either *apologetic* or *apologetically* in the COCA was *smile* as a noun (for *apologetic*) and as a verb (for *apologetically*). Taken together, the gesture expressions fall into four distinct categories: facial expressions (*smile, grimace, grin*), descriptions of gaze (*look, glance*), movements of shoulders and arms (*shrug, gesture, wave*) and head movements (*nod, shake*). All these categories are attested in the data both as silent gestures performing the pragmatic act and as co-speech gestures. Extracts 5.7 to 5.14 provide relevant examples of silent and co-speech gestures for each of the four categories (Jucker 2023: 340, all examples from COCA fiction)

5.7   'Tired?' she asked. He smiled at her, apologetically, and put his hand in his lap.

5.8   Dr McBride looked up at him and smiled again, apologetically this time. 'I'm sorry, Mr Skilling', she said.

5.9   'We all have our own ways of trying to go home', said Sumi, and disappeared from the window's frame, heading off to whatever she'd been doing before Eleanor disturbed her. Eleanor shot Nancy a quick, apologetic look, and then she too was gone, shutting the door behind herself.

5.10 'Maybe Mao Xin could help her get a job', my mother said. (...) 'Sure', I said with an apologetic glance at Lulu.

5.11 Bandar made an apologetic gesture and the old man sniffed and turned to look down the road.

5.12 'Sorry guys.' Liz shrugged apologetically. 'I always tell you that I don't do sports.'

5.13 'He said what?' Drew exclaimed. (...) Raising his voice in the strident way he does when he feels he's being ignored. 'He told other children?' The teacher nodded apologetically.

5.14 As Victor's mother spoke, he nodded apologetically. 'Madam', the captain said when she was finished. 'My sincerest apologies. I will instruct my soldiers to avoid speaking with your boys.'

These examples raise some interesting questions. The first question has to do with the selection of the nonverbal aspects of these pragmatic acts. As we have seen in the previous section, not all visible bodily actions that are described here fall under Kendon's (2004) definition of a gesture. Nodding, shrugging and gesturing appear to be gestures in Kendon's sense while smiling, shooting a look and glancing may be largely inadvertent and, therefore, strictly speaking, outside of Kendon's definition or they may be specifically intended by the communicator to enhance their communicative act. In any case, all of them are elements that are sufficiently salient for the narrators to highlight. As readers, we may assume that the person to whom the apology was addressed recognised the apologetic intent of the gesture even if we do not know in detail what exactly an apologetic smile or glance looks like.

This raises the further question whether such gestures also occur and are recognisable as such outside of fictional contexts. In the fictional context, we have two communicative levels. On the level of the readers, the gestures are assigned a very specific illocutionary point, but on the level of the characters, the illocutionary point may be difficult to perceive. It appears that the gestures derive their illocutionary point for the addressee through their situational context. The extracts 5.7 to 5.14 have been reproduced here with a somewhat limited context, but in each case the pragmatic act appears to take place in a situation in which some offence-remedial action is imminent. In such a situation, a smile, a shrug or any of the other gestures attested in the data may count as apologetic because they contrast sufficiently with alternative non-apologetic gestures that would indicate a disagreement or dispute about the potential offence that led to this particular situation. Intuitively, it seems likely that this is also possible outside of fictional contexts, where there is no narrator to disambiguate the situation, but it is not easy to see how this could be investigated empirically.

We may also ask what the difference is between a fully explicit apology and a maximally vague apologetic gesture and in what situations speakers opt for one rather than the other. This brings us back to the discussion about the relevance of illocutionary indeterminacy in Section 4.4. A maximally vague apology may be the preferred option if the speaker does not want to go on record with an explicit apology that would inevitably entail some self-blame for what has happened. A shrug, a smile or a nod may be sufficient to indicate the apologiser's good intentions and to redress the momentary disbalance created by the offence.

5.4 Gestures and Illocutionary Indeterminacy

It may appear that apologies are special cases. As pointed out in the previous section, it may make sense for a potential apologiser to resort to an apologetic gesture rather than an explicit utterance in order to circumvent possible self-blame. For less inherently face-threatening pragmatic acts this may not be necessary. In order to find out what kind of pragmatic acts are accompanied or carried out by gestures, I carried out an exploratory study in which I changed the search direction. In Jucker (2023), I used the search terms *apologetic* and *apologetically* to search for collocates denoting gestures. For this exploratory project, I used terms denoting gestures as search terms in order to find collocates denoting pragmatic acts. As a starting point, I used ten lexemes that appeared to be promising candidates on the basis of earlier work on similar collocations. They are listed in 5.15 in alphabetical order. They are in capital letters to indicate that each search was carried out both for the noun and the verb. The relevant function of COCA regularly includes related word forms, that is, a search for FROWN as a verb includes *frown*, *frowns*, *frowned* and *frowning*.

5.15 FROWN, GESTURE, GLANCE, HUG, NOD, SHAKE, SHRUG, SMILE, WAVE, WINK

From the resulting lists of collocates, those that were attested at least ten times in COCA were picked out and their frequency noted. The result was a list of 140 distinct gestures – pragmatic act collocations (types) and 6252 individual collocations (tokens). Table 2 provides an overview of the twelve pragmatic acts that appeared most frequently in such collocations.

Table 2 Most frequent collocations of gesture lexemes with lexemes denoting pragmatic acts (derived from COCA and sorted according to collocation frequency)

	NOD	SMILE	GESTURE	SHRUG	WAVE	HUG	GLANCE	SHAKE	FROWN	WINK	total
agree*	963										963
greet*	107	248	30	12	56	84					537
approv*	478	39									517
reply	100	295	11	70						11	487
rueful*	13	282					22	66			383
appreciat*	91	39	226				26				382
apolog*	11	176	25	60	23		33	12			340
dismiss*			71	21	163			11			266
encourag*	104	140				10					254
reassuring*	13	180									193
whisper	95					40	10			15	160
acknowledge*	137										137

*The asterisk stands for different endings. For instance, NOD as a verb collocated with *agreement* (876 times) and *agreeably* (27 times), and NOD as a noun collocated with *agreement* (60 times) to add up to 963 collocations of NOD and *agree**.

The searches for Table 2 were carried out by consulting the lists of collocates that COCA provides for each of the 60,000 most frequent words in its database. This feature does not allow a restriction to a specific section of the corpus, but spot checks confirm that most of these collocations are drawn from the fiction section of the corpus.

According to the figures presented in Table 2, some pragmatic acts collocate regularly with only one or very few gestures. *Agree* and *acknowledge*, for instance, only collocate with *nodding* and *approve* only collocates with *nodding* and *smiling* (irrespective of the part of speech and related word endings). *Greeting* and *apologising*, on the other hand, collocate with six or even seven different gestures. However, the most important insight provided by Table 2 is the fact that two gestures, NOD and SMILE, account for 75 per cent of all the attested individual collocations (across all 6252 collocations of the unabridged version of the table NOD and SMILE account for 70 per cent of all colloca- tions). FROWN, on the other hand, does not collocate with any of the pragmatic acts that are still included in Table 2. It only collocates with *disapprove* and *mutter*, which occur further down in the full table. Thus, nodding and smiling appear to be the most salient gestures that are assigned a communicative intention in connection with a pragmatic act. Extracts 5.16 to 5.24 provide some relevant examples (all examples from COCA Fiction).

5.16   Vanelton grimly nodded agreement.

5.17   five young plainclothes policemen nodded polite greetings to the commissario

5.18   he nodded in approval and said, 'You are correct, sir'.

5.19   'Oh, I understand?' Evelyn replied, nodding.

5.20   She smiled brightly and greeted Nathan.

5.21   'Thank you, Mr. Hawthorn', she replied politely, smiling.

5.22   Kally squeezed her hand and smiled encouragingly.

5.23   I shake my head. 'Too expensive.' She smiles ruefully. 'Not tonight.'

5.24   The old woman smiled at him reassuringly. 'Doctor will be in after breakfast',

The examples show that the gestures are sometimes performed silently and sometimes they are accompanied by speech. Extract 5.23 appears to be a special case. Here the collocate denoting a pragmatic act is the adverb *ruefully*. The corresponding verb 'to rue' does not appear to be a regular speech act verb, but the adjective *rueful* and the adverb *ruefully* appear to be used in very similar ways to *apologetic* and *apologetically*.

Table 3 shows how such fictional examples can be placed systematically on a scale of illocutionary explicitness. The table shows three examples and provides four different extracts for each. They differ in terms of their illocutionary

Table 3 Scale of illocutionary explicitness (all examples from COCA Fiction)

	PA including explicit performative	PA including IPID + gesture	PA without IPID + gesture	Silent gesture
Apologise	'Okay then, my mistake, I apologize.'	Her smile was apologetic. 'Sorry, I gotta go.'	'Mine's short', the woman said, smiling apologetically.	He smiled at her, apologetically.
Rue	'I regret that I haven't been able to pay you.'	She gave me a rueful smile. 'Sorry.'	'I might as well', he said with a rueful smile.	He plucked at his beard and gave in to a rueful smile.
Thank	'I want to thank you for helping me see things clear.'	'Thanks.' Tamia smiled gratefully at Brandon.	'So you have returned!' Yasmine said, smiling gratefully.	Gary smiled gratefully at her in return.
Communicative act	Maximally explicit (illocutionary point encoded)	⟵	⟶	Maximally vague (for characters)
Responsibility for illocution assignment	Character	⟵	⟶	Narrator
Showing vs telling	Mainly showing	⟵	⟶	Mainly telling

explicitness. In the first column, the illustrations contain reported speech in which one character indicates explicitly what the illocutionary point of the utterance is by using an explicit performative, *I apologise*, *I regret*, and *I want to thank you*. In terms of a pragmatics of fiction, it is the character who takes responsibility for the illocution that is expressed. The author uses the showing mode with little or no narratorial mediation. The reader witnesses the event directly (Locher and Jucker 2021: 127). In the second column, there is a combination of showing and telling. The verbal pragmatic act includes an illocutionary point indicating device, such as *sorry* or *thanks*. The pragmatic act is still highly explicit as to its illocutionary point, but it is accompanied by a gesture with an illocutionary point (apologetic, rueful, gratefully). The third column also contains examples that combine showing and telling, but in these cases, the verbal pragmatic act is less explicit. It does not include an IPID and might be ambiguous for the addressed character. The reader derives the illocutionary point of the utterance mainly through the telling mode. In the last column, the gesture is performed silently. The narrator is in overt control of how the situation is presented (Locher and Jucker 2021: 127).

In conclusion, we can see that fictional texts provide an excellent source for a preliminary investigation into the multimodality of pragmatic acts. They provide a first-order perspective of what gestures are salient in their communicative potential. Nodding and smiling stand out as the most frequent ones in the data. They go together with a large range of different pragmatic acts. Authors of fictional texts regularly use gesture descriptions as a device in the telling mode to disambiguate the illocutionary potential of what characters do for their readers.

6 'O, Cry You Mercy, Sir; I Have Mistook': The Diachronicity of Speech Acts

This section explores the diachronicity of speech acts. It will survey the research methods that are needed to identify and retrieve specific speech acts from historical sources. The focus will be on meta-illocutionary expressions and their potential for retrieving the speech acts that they denote as well as the technique of using small sample corpora to manually establish relevant manifestations of a specific speech act, which can then be used for automatic retrievals in large corpora. In addition, this section also discusses the challenges of tracing long-term trajectories of specific speech acts, that is, the development of, for instance, apologies from the earliest extant sources to the present day.

6.1 Apologies Now and Then

Extracts 6.1 to 6.3 provide examples of apologies across Early Modern, Late Modern and Present-day English.

6.1   Julia (as Sebastian): O, cry you mercy, sir; I have mistook: Why, this is the ring you sent to Silvia. (Shakespeare, *The Two Gentlemen of Verona*, 5.4.91)

6.2   Edward Erskine: I called, Mrs. Wilson, to ask of you the favour of Miss Elton's company to-morrow on the bridal escort.
Mrs. Wilson: I am sorry that any young woman's manners, who is brought up in my house, should authorize a gentleman to believe she will, of course, ride with him if asked.
Edward Erskine: I beg your pardon, madam, I have been so happy as to obtain Miss Elton's consent, subject to yours.
(COHA, Fic, 1825)

6.3   Question. Can I make a full back up of this in case I need to install it at later date if my box does a wobbly? I've tried USB to SD Add-on (can't remember exact name soz) (iWeb)

In 6.1, Julia disguised as Proteus' page, Sebastian, apologises for having confused two rings, the one that she received herself in her true identity as Julia and one that she, in her role as page, was supposed to take to Silvia. In 6.2, Edward Erskine appears to apologise to Mrs. Wilson for disagreeing with her. And in 6.3, a blogger apologises with *soz*, an abbreviated form of *sorry*, for not being able to supply the name of the SD Add-on that he or she mentions in connection to a computer problem. Corpus sources do not always provide enough context to give a full interpretation of what exactly is going on. For a detailed interpretation, we need to know what exactly the offence is that the apologiser apologises for. Whether it was a big offence or only a minor one. Whether the apologiser is serious about the apology and contrite about what has happened as in Extract 6.2, whether there is an ironic twist to the apology as in Extract 6.1 or whether it is just a mock apology as in Extract 6.3. It may well be, for instance, that Julia disguised as Sebastian mixed up the two rings on purpose in order to expose Proteus' infidelity and therefore only pretends to be sorry for the confusion that she has created by first showing the ring that she had received.

We have seen in the previous sections, that the fuzziness of the illocutionary point and the variability of the illocutionary force is an inherent feature of pragmatic acts (see in particular Section 4). For some pragmatic acts, the variability may be greater than for others which are perhaps more standardised and less problematic than apologies. As we have seen, this poses multiple challenges for their analysis. In a historical context, however, these problems are exacerbated.

It is not clear, for instance, whether earlier generations of language users availed themselves of the same inventory of pragmatic acts. Given the multifaceted changes in the social fabric and communication technology, it seems plausible to assume that there must have been some significant changes in our communicative needs and therefore in the strategies we deal with them. But we do not have access to native speaker intuition of earlier centuries and therefore have to rely entirely on empirical research tools. We can look at manifestations of pragmatic acts in the many different sources that have come down to us (more about them later) and we can investigate the meta-illocutionary lexicon of earlier periods which provides us with a first-order perspective on those pragmatic acts that were sufficiently salient for speakers, or rather writers, of those periods to name them and to talk about them.

In the process, we always have to bear in mind that the meta-illocutionary lexicon can be deceptive. If we start with a meta-illocutionary expression that we are familiar with in Present-day English and we find this expression at a certain point in the history of English, we might prematurely conclude that both the meta-illocutionary expression and the pragmatic act remained more or less unchanged. Alternatively, we might find that the expression itself has a relatively short history and conclude that the designated pragmatic act had an equally short history in the English language. Chances are that both these conclusions are wrong. The meta-illocutionary lexicon has changed over the centuries and the nature of the pragmatic acts that are designated with its expressions has changed, too. More specifically, as I will show in Section 6.3, apologies have a long history, but their nature changed quite drastically. In Anglo-Saxon times, the closest equivalent that we have attested in the surviving texts consist of penitential acts of confession to God while today we have a whole range of apologetic moves ranging from the deep and heartfelt expression of regret to a perfunctory spill cry with dubious credentials as to its apologetic point. The meta-illocutionary expression *apology*, however, is more recent. According to the *Oxford English Dictionary* it was first attested in 1533.

Given these problems, a historical analysis of pragmatic acts has to deal with two major challenges. First, how can specific pragmatic acts be traced in historical corpora and second, how can their developments over time be analysed given the fuzzy nature of both the pragmatic acts themselves and the meta-illocutionary lexicon.

6.2 Tracing Speech Acts in Historical Corpora

Historical pragmatics is the field of research that investigates patterns of language use of the past and how these patterns changed over time and as such it is the field that is interested in the history of speech acts (see Jucker and

Taavitsainen 2013 and Brinton 2023 for overviews). Like all other fields of historical linguistics, historical pragmatics generally has to rely on written material that has survived from the past. This appears to be a rather obvious statement, but it has considerable consequences for the historical linguist and not all of these consequences may be equally obvious. The data limitations are increasingly severe the further back a researcher goes in the history of a language. For English, the first written records go back to the eighth century, a time when very few people knew how to read and write. Writing was a specialised skill used for a very small range of communicative needs, and only a few of the documents that were written at the time survived the vagaries of time to still be accessible to us today. Over the centuries, the percentage of literate people as well as the communicative needs for written texts increased. But it is important to remember that in spite of the many historical corpora that we have at our disposal today, our access to the language of the past is seriously and systematically distorted. In the early centuries, religious texts and legal texts predominated and they were mostly written by men in religious orders and from the highest social ranks. A present-day corpus that relied on the same range of texts and authors would, of course, be deemed to be entirely unsuitable to represent a present-day language, but for Old English, that is, texts written between about 800 and 1150, this is more or less what we have and it is always good to remember that this is what generalisations about pragmatic acts or any other aspect of language are based on. For later periods, the situation changes and generally improves in terms of text genres that have survived, but each period has its own limitations and they must be borne in mind in the context of historical pragmatics.

For the very recent past, there are recordings that are available for historical pragmatic investigations, for example, radio broadcasts or parliamentary proceedings. Such sources give direct access to the spoken word of past decades reaching back to the middle of the twentieth century and even earlier. Early recordings of the spoken word are generally severely restricted in the scope of registers that are easily available in sufficient quantity, but some work has already been carried out on such sources (for example, Jucker and Landert 2015; Reber 2021; Reber and Jucker 2023). In addition, corpora have recently become available that contain written versions of spoken language going back almost one hundred years, as, for instance, the *Movie Corpus* and the *TV Corpus*, which go back to the 1930s and 1950s, respectively. These sources are far from perfect for pragmatic investigations because they rely on subtitles rather than careful transcriptions, but they have proved useful for some investigations in recent pragmatic changes in the spoken language.

In the early days of historical pragmatics, in the 1990s and 2000s, researchers were concerned about the oral nature of their data. As a result, they gave preference to data that could be argued to be as close as possible to the spoken language of the past. Theatre plays, transcriptions of courtroom proceedings and private correspondence were all considered in their own ways to be less than perfect but sufficiently good approximations because they consisted of fictional imitations of spoken language, transcripts of actual spoken language and interactions that were conversation-like in spite of their written modality. More recently, such reservations about the written modality of historical sources have given way to a realisation that all language modalities are communicative and therefore provide equally valid data for pragmatic theorising provided the nature of the data is always part of the pragmatic analysis. Theatre plays, therefore, to take just one example, are a valid source to investigate how playwrights chose to represent face-to-face interactions, but they should not be taken to be imperfect approximations to the 'real' thing, that is, everyday spoken language.

For historical data, preliminary explorations into specific pragmatic acts were carried out with the methods called illustrative and structural eclecticism by Kohnen (2015; see also Brinton 2023: 133). Under the first heading, Kohnen subsumes speech act studies that do not rely on a corpus in a strict sense. Instead, they use examples drawn from various sources to illustrate a particular speech act at different points in the history of a language. Arnovick (1999), one of the pioneers of historical speech act studies, for instance, investigated the history of insults, promises, curses, greetings, farewells and sneeze blessings in the history of English. Many of these individual speech act histories are illustrated with no more than a handful of carefully selected examples from a variety of historical and mostly fictional sources. The development of the blessing *God be with you* that turned into the present-day *goodbye* is a notable exception as it is based on a more systematic corpus study in the *Chadwyck-Healy* drama collection. This already leads to the approaches that are called structural eclecticism by Kohnen. They search more systematically for specific manifestations of speech acts in historical corpora, such as the *Helsinki Corpus*, *ARCHER*, the *Chadwyck-Healy* drama and fiction collection or the *Corpus of Historical American English*. Taavitsainen and Jucker (2008), for instance, searched for compliments in the *Chadwyck-Healy* drama and fiction collection with the help of the speech act verb *compliment* and with a range of positive adjectives. And Jucker and Taavitsainen (2008) searched for phrases, such as *excuse me, pardon me, I beg your pardon* or *I am sorry* in order to retrieve apologies from the same source. With this method, many relevant examples can be retrieved from the corpus, but it is clear that many more instances of the same speech act will have been missed.

More systematic historical studies of individual speech acts rely on the methodologies introduced in Section 3 (see Figure 1), where four different research approaches have been distinguished, that is, the search for manifestations of specific speech acts via the search for illocutionary point indicating devices or for typical patterns and the search for meta-illocutionary expressions as an end in itself or as a proxy for finding manifestations of the named illocution in close proximity of the expression.

Kohnen (2007, 2008) has worked out a methodology for tracing specific speech acts more systematically in historical corpora. This method relies on a restriction to specific genres, for example, sermons, private letters or prayers, which are attested throughout the period under investigation and which keep the communicative situation and text function relatively stable across time. From such genre-specific corpora, he draws reasonably sized sample corpora throughout the entire period covered by the main corpus and uses these samples for a manual search of all manifestations of a specific speech act, as for instance directives. Given a careful selection of samples that are sufficiently large but still manageable, the method will produce a reasonably comprehensive inventory of manifestations of directives that can be expected in the entire corpus. To the extent that these manifestations can be turned into specific search strings, it is possible to retrieve them from the entire corpus and use them for detailed statistics of their developments over time. This procedure may still miss a few manifestations of directives, but it has a good chance of retrieving most patterns with a reasonable frequency of occurrence in the entire corpus.

Jucker (2018) combined two different approaches to trace apologies in the *Corpus of Historical American English* from 1810 to 2009. On the one hand, he used illocutionary point indicating devices, such as *sorry, excuse, apologise* and *pardon* to search for those apologies that use these expressions and on the other hand, he used the meta-illocutionary expression *apology* and its morphological variants to retrieve passages in which speakers explicitly talk about apologies. Both methods require extensive manual coding of the retrieved hits and careful interrater reliability tests to make sure that the coding is consistent across time and neither of them can be expected to uncover all the apologies in the corpus. The search for IPIDs is likely to miss very indirect or unusual formulations of apologies while the search for meta-illocutionary expressions is likely to miss more casual and routine apologies because it focuses on passages in which speakers see a need to talk about this pragmatic act or to use the expression performatively in a particularly explicit apology. However, together the two methods provide an interesting line of development of apologies across two centuries of American English. It turns out that the frequency of apologies increases considerably during this period. They get increasingly conventionalised and the IPID *sorry* multiplies in frequency. At the beginning of the nineteenth century, it is one among several others, by the end of the twentieth century it accounts for about three quarters of all apology expressions while *excuse* as the second most frequent one accounts for no more than 10 per cent (Jucker 2018: 387).

A more comprehensive approach avoiding the shortcomings described above was chosen by Culpeper and Archer (2008), who investigated requests in the *Sociopragmatic Corpus* consisting of play texts and trial proceedings from 1640 to 1760 and containing some 220,000 words. In this relatively small corpus, they coded every single one of about 9,500 utterances in terms of speaker and addressee demographics (gender, social status, age) and its possible status as a direct or indirect request. This allows for a very detailed and fine-grained analysis of different types of requests, including indirect ones, across the two different genres of the *Sociopragmatic Corpus*. The results show that late Early Modern English requests are very different from those described by Blum-Kulka and House (1989: 134) in Present-day English, German, French, Hebrew and Spanish. In each of these present-day languages, conventionally indirect formulations predominated, while in Culpeper and Archer's late Early Modern English data it was the impositives that accounted for almost 80 per cent of all requests. However, Blum-Kulka and House's results are based on discourse completion tasks while Culpeper and Archer used play texts and trial proceedings as their data. It is an open question to what extent these data sources are directly comparable.

6.3 Long-Term Speech Act Trajectories

Speech acts have been investigated both from a historical and a diachronic perspective. Researchers are interested both in the form and function of specific pragmatic acts at a given period in the history of a language and in the diachronic development of pragmatic acts over time. However, this field of research is still relatively young while the study of changes in the sound system, morphology, syntax and semantics have always been core areas of historical linguistics and much is known about the systematicity of changes on these levels. On the level of pragmatic changes and in particular for pragmatic acts, we have no more than a selection of partial histories for some particularly salient pragmatic acts that have caught the curiosity of historical pragmaticists (for a brief overview of a number of such histories see Brinton 2023: chapter 6). This is not yet enough for a solid theory of pragmatic change that can be generalised across large inventories of pragmatic acts or even across all of them. But some attempts have already been made to find generalisations for speech act trajectories.

Two different perspectives can be distinguished in these endeavours; a form-to-function approach and a function-to-form approach (see Jacobs and Jucker 1995 for the origin of this terminological distinction). In a form-to-function approach, the researcher starts with a particular word or phrase and investigates their diachronically changing functions while a function-to-form approach focuses on a specific speech function and traces its diachronically changing manifestations. Given the fuzziness of speech acts and the fact that diachronically both the form and the function of any given linguistic entity are likely to change, the distinction is often difficult to maintain and only serves heuristic purposes.

However, Claridge and Arnovick (2010: 183) focus mainly on a form-to-function approach when they talk about discursisation as a pathway of development of the farewell greeting *goodbye* and the sneeze blessing *bless you*. These developments have to be seen against the background of the process of pragmaticalisation, which describes a type of change that turns lexical material into a pragmatic element. The discourse marker *well*, for instance, historically derives from the adverb *well*, the interjection *gee* from the proper noun *Jesus*, and the Early Modern English courtesy markers *pray* and *prithee* from a matrix clause. In the case of *goodbye* and *bless you*, however, pragmatic elements derive from other pragmatic elements in a process that Claridge and Arnovick (2010) call discursisation. They both have an illocutionary rather than a propositional function at the beginning of the process. The conversational formula *goodbye* derives from the phrase *God be with you* that is regularly attested in Early Modern English at the end of a dialogue, for instance in a play, where it counted both as a blessing and as a courteous way of closing the interaction. Presumably, blessings were common at the end of dialogues and therefore had this secondary illocution of closing the dialogue. Starting in the late sixteenth century, the phrase underwent contraction and eventually merged into one word, *goodbye*, where the element *good* is substituted for the element *God*. At the same time, the closing function became increasingly dominant. There may even have been some influence through the analogy of *good-day* that helped this substitution. At the end of the nineteenth century, the process had progressed so far that the phrase could no longer be used as a blessing and *God be with you* reappears in the data for cases of actual blessings (Claridge and Arnovick 2010: 175–76; and for a more comprehensive account Arnovick 1999: chapter 6). The conversational formula *bless you* that is sometimes uttered as a response to somebody sneezing has undergone a similar development from what originally was a religious blessing with slightly more complex forms (*we ðec bletsiaþ*, Old English, 'we bless you'; or *blessed mote þow be*, Middle English, 'you may be blessed') to a superstitious blessing and finally into a wish or a mere polite formula that for many has lost its religious component entirely (Claridge and Arnovick 2010: 177, Arnovick 1999: chapter 7). The term discursisation, therefore, designates a pathway of change for these two, and possibly other, cases of linguistic expressions that change their illocutionary point in the course of time while the expressions themselves undergo a process of contraction.

Jucker (2019), on the other hand, starts out from a particular illocutionary function, apologising, and traces its manifestations from Old English to Present-day English. He argues that apologies originate in Old English penitential acts and confessions to God and in a process of what he calls attenuation, develop into the fully pragmaticalised and minimalised apologies that we are familiar with in Present-day English (see Figure 5).

Based on Kohnen (2017) and Williamson (2018), he argues that apologies in a modern sense are not attested or referred to in the data that has survived from Old English. Instead, there are passages in which speakers address themselves to God in order to express regret for their sins and to ask for forgiveness. In the Middle English period, passages can be found in which such speech acts of remorse are addressed not to God but to a fellow Christian who is asked for forgiveness. In the late Middle English and Early Modern English period, there is increasing evidence of a secularisation of apologies and it is at this point that the term apology is first attested in the English language (Jucker 2019: 13). But they are still relatively complex and often include terms of address and prefatory phrases, such as *I hope*, *I pray you* or *I beseech you*, as in Extract 6.4.

6.4   Most gracious Princesse, how much I grieve to see your discomfort, J cannot say, but hope your Grace will pardon me, which have been more bold (presuming on your favour) then beseemeth me.
(LION; Anon, Marianvs (c. 1641): chap. XVII, page 159; quoted from Jucker and Taavitsainen 2008: 238)

According to Jucker (2019: 14), apologies still tend to be more complex in the early nineteenth century than they often are today, but they show signs of

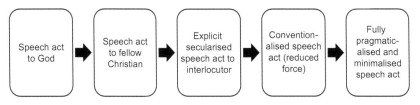

Figure 5 Scale of speech act attenuation (based on Jucker 2019: 7)

increasing conventionalisation and at the same time their force often seems to be reduced. The illocutionary point indicating device *sorry* starts to take over as the most important apology expression whilst *pardon*, *forgive* and *excuse* are more and more backgrounded. In Present-day English, finally, apologies are often no more than token acknowledgements for minor infractions. They are regularly performed by a mere *sorry* or even by spill cries such as *oops* or *whoops*. Thus, in the course of time, apologies have undergone a process of attenuation, that is, a weakening of their force and at the same time their manifestations underwent a process of conventionalisation and minimalisation. These new forms, however, have not ousted the more elaborate and more creative forms. What has happened is that the spectrum of apologies has opened up and led to a co-existence of maximally sincere and heartfelt apologies with maximally attenuated and reduced ones and everything between these two extremes.

7 Open Issues and Outlook

The final section brings together the threads of the previous sections by looking at the four waves of speech act research again and how they compare to each other in terms of a second-order perspective, that is, speech acts defined by the researcher on the basis of felicity conditions and a first order perspective, that is, speech act labels used by the language users themselves on the basis of their importance and saliency for everyday communication. The second part of this section highlights promising research directions for future work on speech acts. It focuses mainly on the multimodality and historicity of speech acts and on some of the research challenges that they present.

7.1 Where We Are

The first three sections of this Element provided some of the foundations of speech act theory, its early developments and an overview of relevant research tools. These early developments were presented in terms of the first three waves of speech act theory, in which the very first wave comprises the work by the language philosophers Austin and Searle and the early adaptations of their work within pragmatics (e.g., Levinson 1983: chapter 5). It was based on the philosophers' research tools of introspection and careful analysis of what it means to perform verbal actions or – to use Austin's (1962) famous book title – how to do things with words. This work had a lasting impact and some of the basic concepts and terminologies continue to be useful even today. The second and the third wave of speech act research moved from introspection to empirical investigations. The second wave used various types of elicitation experiments and naturally occurring contrastive situations in order to explore different ways of performing the same speech act, focusing mainly on speaker demographics. Speakers of different languages or different varieties of the same language were compared. Learner varieties were compared with native speaker varieties, and so on. The third wave rejected elicitation experiments in favour of large corpora of authentic language data. In the process, the focus on speaker demographics was largely replaced by a focus on the question of how speech acts are performed in different linguistic contexts, for example, in different registers or in different time periods. The third wave, for the first time, allowed a systematic extension of speech act research into historical periods opening up a large spectrum of new research questions about earlier manifestations of speech acts and about trajectories of their development over time.

The first three waves of speech act theory and research continue to be of importance even today. The philosophical foundations still inform some of our thinking on speech acts and both the experimental and the corpus-based tradition are well represented in many publications today. The methods continue to be modified and adapted to offer new insights and to avoid some of the criticisms levelled at the early versions of these methods.

The fourth wave of speech act research, however, constitutes a somewhat bigger step away from the early approaches. Sections 4, 5 and 6 were devoted to different aspects of this fourth wave. Section 4 looked at the discursive nature of speech acts, that is, the way in which speech acts can be understood as a joint production of the speaker and the addressee. Speech acts are fuzzy entities. Their illocutionary point may be explicitly encoded, for example, with an illocutionary point indicating device or underspecified and vague. Whether explicit and clear or underspecified, the addressee either (silently) accepts the illocutionary point as sufficiently clear for current purposes or in need of some explicit negotiations. Section 5 looked at the multimodal nature of speech acts, which in this context should be called pragmatic acts. While it is intuitively obvious that specific pragmatic acts owe much of their communicative potential to the nonverbal aspects of their delivery, the research tools that we have today appear to be in their early stages of development. The section mainly looked at those multimodal aspects that are sufficiently salient for speakers, or writers, to explicitly comment about them. And Section 6, finally, was devoted to the historicity of speech acts. Historical accounts always need to take into account the limited nature of the data that has survived. Earlier centuries had communicative needs that differ from ours and writing was more marginal than it is today, which makes straightforward comparisons difficult. But even beyond these difficulties, it is not easy to capture speech acts – or pragmatic acts – used hundreds of years ago and compare them with what we are doing today. The section has shown that both the form and the function of these entities is likely to have changed substantially.

A comparison of the first three waves with the fourth wave reveals several important aspects. While the first three waves considered speech acts to be entities that could be captured by well-defined felicity conditions, the fourth wave has to come to terms with the indeterminate nature of speech acts. The first three waves focused mainly on the utterance produced by a speaker and the inherent features of this utterance. The fourth wave, in contrast, focuses on speech acts as a negotiated entity produced by the speaker and the addressee in cooperation. The most important difference between the first three waves and the fourth lies in the perspective taken on the definition of specific speech acts. In the first three waves, the researchers relied largely on speech act definitions provided through felicity conditions. Thus, even in the empirical work of the second and the third wave, the basis has been provided by philosophical tools of introspection to identify specific speech acts in the data. The researchers created situations in which specific speech acts – according to the researchers' definitions – were likely to occur or they searched corpora for instances of specific speech acts, again using pre-determined definitions. As a result, the three waves focused almost exclusively on prototypical speech acts, that is, speech acts whose illocutionary point was as clear and unambiguous as possible. The fourth wave, on the other hand, focuses much more on a first-order perspective, that is, the perspective taken by the language users. It investigates those speech actions that are sufficiently salient for language users to explicitly talk about them.

The two perspectives complement each other in obvious ways. A second-order perspective provides meticulous analytical tools for well-defined entities. This is essential if large numbers of speech acts of the same type are to be compared across different speakers or across different contexts of occurrence. A first-order perspective, on the other hand, captures the variable nature of how language users think about certain speech acts. Not everybody agrees on what an apology is, for instance. Which situations call for an apology? How sincere does an apology have to be? And what makes an apology an adequate apology? Such a first-order perspective focuses on the fuzzy nature of speech acts and on what is salient for a particular speech community.

7.2 And Where We Are Going

One of the basic problems that has vexed speech act theorists for a long time is the issue of whether it is possible to establish a comprehensive list of all speech acts of any given language. Levinson (2015: 205) considers the different positions taken by earlier scholars, that is, Austin's position that speech acts are basically cultural in nature and hence part of an open-ended list and Grice's position that speech act types are based on two propositional attitudes of wanting and judging. Searle's five large classes of speech acts form a middle position, that is, representatives (e.g., assertions), directives (i.e., attempts to get the addressee to do something), commissives (i.e., commitments by the speaker to do something), expressives (such as thanking and apologising) and declarations (such as blessing and christening). Levinson rejects this classification on the grounds that it ignores many of the actions identified by conversation analysts. He lists continuers, such as *hmhm*, repair initiators and repair responses as relevant examples. According to Levinson, the classification also fails to account for culture-bound special cases. As an example, he cites an exchange of father-in-law jokes in Yélî Dnye, a Papuan culture, which apparently defy a classification according to Searle's categories. It is clear that these examples constitute second-order definitions of specific speech acts, that is, speech actions that are recognised as such by the researcher even if they do not have a vernacular name and therefore do not appear to be salient enough for the speakers of the language to name them and to talk about them.

The search for an inventory of speech acts, therefore, must specify clearly whether it searches for first-order or second-order entities. Levinson's reservations about the possibility to establish a comprehensive repertoire (of second-order entities) seem plausible. Future research is likely to propose new distinctions and to identify new speech actions. A list of second-order speech acts, therefore, is unlikely to be finite in principle. The search for first-order speech acts, on the other hand, will identify speech act verbs that are by definition language and culture specific. Attempts to theorise such lists of speech act verbs have a long history. They go back to the early days of speech act research within pragmatics (see for instance Verschueren 1985, 1994 and Traugott 1991).

A better understanding of the scope and the extent of the repertoire of speech act verbs would help us in the discursive approaches to speech acts. In the early days of speech act research, the choice of specific speech acts for investigation was largely informed by their potential to create face threats either for the speaker or for the addressee. And much of the work since then has continued to look at apologies, directives, complaints and compliments. A more systematic assessment of the inventory of first-order speech act labels would help us to set the choice of speech acts to be investigated on a more solid empirical foundation.

Another area of considerable potential for further research concerns their multimodality. Section 5 took a first-order perspective to look at salient gestures and facial expressions. This needs to be extended empirically to non-fictional situations. Recent years have seen a growing interest in the multimodal nature of communication (see the handbooks by Müller et al. 2013 and Müller et al. 2014 and more recently Jucker, Hübscher and Brown 2023). Studies that focus on the multimodality of specific speech actions are still rare, but some work in this area has recently been published. Hübscher et al. (2023), for instance, investigate the multimodality of requests in Catalan. They used discourse elicitation tasks to study how Catalan speakers use facial and body cues when producing a request in polite and in non-polite contexts and the results show that more gestural mitigation strategies are used in polite contexts than in non-polite contexts. And Fang (2023) looks at the multimodal cues that are used by groups of Chinese and Indonesian speakers using English as a lingua franca in role plays that elicit refusals. The study shows that body position, smiling voices, smiling facial expressions and gaze aversion play an important role in the maintenance of rapport when mitigating the force of refusals. Such studies clearly demonstrate that our gestures and facial expressions are an important part of our communicative acts. They are attuned to contextual factors, such as levels of politeness even if we are not always consciously aware of their impact on the interaction between speaker and addressee. The first-order perspective provided in Section 5 focuses on the more prominent aspects of gestures and facial expressions, those that are salient enough to be picked up by narrators as part of their narrative accounts, while the research by Hübscher et al. (2023) and Fang (2023) tries to tease out the subtleties that tend to escape our conscious awareness. Both perspectives offer a wealth of new and exciting research opportunities, but they force us to expand the research methods and the descriptive tools in order to capture the details of how people communicate beyond the spoken words.

As pointed out in Section 6, there are already a considerable number of studies investigating selected speech acts in historical periods, but this is just a beginning. Even for well-researched Indo-European languages, such as English, Spanish, French, German and Dutch, or for Chinese and for Japanese we have no more than a few illustrative investigations of selected speech acts in their historical contexts. For less well-researched languages the situation is more serious. This opens up research opportunities in several directions. As a basis, more studies of individual speech acts for specific historical periods in specific languages are needed. A rich inventory of such studies will enable cross-linguistic investigations comparing specific speech acts or families of speech acts, across different languages. Some work in this area has already been carried out. Taavitsainen and Włodarczyk (2021), for instance, investigated insults in translations of Shakespeare's *Othello* into German, Swedish, Polish and Finnish. And House et al. (2023) studied closings in nineteenth-century letters in English, German and Chinese. There are endless opportunities for specific language pairs or groups of languages to be compared in terms of specific speech act realisations, but needless to say that such comparisons always require a careful consideration of the tertium comparationis, that is, the common denominator that makes the entities under investigation comparable across different languages (see Taavitsainen and Włodarczyk 2021: 170 for details).

An additional direction of research combines series of historical accounts of a particular speech act into long-term trajectories of speech act developments. In Section 6, I provided an outline of the history of apologies that started out in the Anglo-Saxon period as penitential acts and confessions to God and underwent a process of attenuation to become what they are today (Jucker 2019). Such trajectories obviously depend on detailed knowledge about the individual stages across the centuries and so far, not many speech acts have been investigated in sufficient historical detail to allow for convincing descriptions of their long-term trajectories. With the availability of additional trajectories, it will be possible to compare them and find generalisations across different trajectories of the same language or even generalisation of trajectories across different languages. In the area of semantic change, we already have a reasonable number of case studies that allow the identification of regularities of how the meaning of words tends to change diachronically (see, in particular, Traugott and Dasher 2005). In the area of historical speech act research, we are still a long way off from a similar level of understanding of the relevant developments. This offers endless research opportunities for future generations of researchers.

Data Sources, Corpora and Dictionary

ARCHER. A Representative Corpus of Historical English Registers. ARCHER Consortium. (1993–). www.projects.alc.manchester.ac.uk/archer/.

British National Corpus. BNC Consortium. (1991–). www.natcorp.ox.ac.uk/.

Chadwyck-Healy Literature Collections. https://collections.chadwyck.com/

Corpus of Contemporary American English (COCA). Davies, Mark. (2008–). www.english-corpora.org/coca/.

Corpus of English Dialogues 1560–1760. Kytö, Merja and Culpeper, Jonathan. (2006). Oxford Text Archive, http://hdl.handle.net/20.500.12024/2507.

Corpus of Historical American English (COHA). Davies, Mark. (2010). www.english-corpora.org/coha/.

Helsinki Corpus. (1991). Oxford Text Archive, http://hdl.handle.net/20.500.12024/1477. (2011). https://helsinkicorpus.arts.gla.ac.uk/display.py?what=index.

ICE-Ireland. www.ice-corpora.uzh.ch/en/joinice/Teams/iceire.html

International Corpus of English. (1990–). www.ice-corpora.uzh.ch/en.html.

Kun, Michael and Susan Mullen. (2016). *We are Still Tornadoes*. New York: St. Martin's Press.

London-Lund Corpus of Spoken English. (1990). Svartvik, Jan. Oxford Text Archive. http://hdl.handle.net/20.500.12024/0168.

Oxford English Dictionary. www.oed.com.

Santa Barbara Corpus of Spoken American English (SBCSAE). Du Bois, John W., Wallace L. Chafe and Charles Meyer, et al. (2000–2005). https://www.linguistics.ucsb.edu/research/santa-barbara-corpus

Sociopragmatic Corpus: A Specialised Sub-section of A Corpus of English Dialogues 1560–1760. Compiled by Jonathan Culpeper and Dawn Archer. Lancaster: Department of Linguistics and English Language, Lancaster University.

SPICE-Ireland. Kirk, John M. and Jeffrey L. Kallen (2011). https://johnmkirk.etinu.net/cgi-bin/generic?instanceID=11.

References

Aijmer, Karin. (1996). *Conversational Routines in English: Convention and Creativity*. London: Longman.

Anchimbe, Eric A. (2018). *Offers and Offer Refusals: A Postcolonial Pragmatics Perspective on World Englishes*. (Pragmatics and Beyond New Series 298). Amsterdam: John Benjamins.

Arnovick, Leslie K. (1999). *Diachronic Pragmatics: Seven Case Studies in English Illocutionary Development*. (Pragmatics and Beyond New Series 68). Amsterdam: John Benjamins.

Assimakopoulos, Stavros. (in press). *Speech Acts: Linguistic and Social Perspectives*. (Cambridge Elements). Cambridge: Cambridge University Press.

Austin, J. L. (1962). *How to Do Things with Words: The William James Lectures Delivered at Harvard University in 1955*. Oxford: Oxford University Press.

Blum-Kulka, Shoshana and Juliane House. (1989). Cross-cultural and situational variation in requesting behavior. In Shoshana Blum-Kulka, Juliane House and Gabriele Kasper (eds.). *Cross-Cultural Pragmatics: Requests and Apologies*. Norwood, NJ: Ablex, pp. 123–154.

Blum-Kulka, Shoshana, Juliane House and Gabriele Kasper, (eds.). (1989). *Cross-Cultural Pragmatics: Requests and Apologies*. Norwood, NJ: Ablex.

Brinton, Laurel J. (2023). *Pragmatics in the History of English*. Cambridge: Cambridge University Press.

Brown, Penelope and Stephen C. Levinson. (1987). *Politeness: Some Universals in Language Usage*. (Studies in Interactional Sociolinguistics 4). Cambridge: Cambridge University Press.

Chang, Wei-Lin Melody and Michael Haugh. (2011). Evaluations of im/politeness of an intercultural apology. *Intercultural Pragmatics* 8.3, 411–442.

Claridge, Claudia and Leslie Arnovick. (2010). Pragmaticalisation and discursisation. In Andreas H. Jucker and Irma Taavitsainen (eds.). *Historical Pragmatics*. (Handbooks of Pragmatics 8). Berlin: De Gruyter Mouton, pp. 165–192.

Couper-Kuhlen, Elizabeth and Margret Selting. (2018). *Interactional Linguistics: An Introduction to Language in Social Interaction*. Cambridge: Cambridge University Press.

Culpeper, Jonathan. (2011). *Impoliteness: Using Language to Cause Offence*. Cambridge: Cambridge University Press.

Culpeper, Jonathan and Dawn Archer. (2008). Requests and directness in Early Modern English trial proceedings and play texts, 1640–1760. In Andreas H. Jucker and Irma Taavitsainen (eds.). *Speech Acts in the History of English*. (Pragmatics and Beyond New Series 176). Amsterdam: John Benjamins, pp. 45–84.

Culpeper, Jonathan and Michael Haugh. (2014). *Pragmatics and the English Language*. London: Palgrave Macmillan.

Deutschmann, Mats. (2003). *Apologising in British English*. (Skrifter från moderna språk 10). Umeå: Institutionen för Moderna språk, Umeå University.

Fang, Xianming. (2023). Multimodality in refusals in English as a lingua franca. In Andreas H. Jucker, Iris Hübscher and Lucien Brown (eds.). *Multimodal Im/politeness: Signed, Spoken, Written*. (Pragmatics and Beyond New Series 333). Amsterdam: John Benjamins, pp. 101–129.

Félix-Brasdefer, J. César. (2015). *The Language of Service Encounters: A Pragmatic-Discursive Approach*. Cambridge: Cambridge University Press.

Félix-Brasdefer, J. César. (2018). Role plays. In Andreas H. Jucker, Klaus P. Schneider and Wolfram Bublitz (eds.). *Methods in Pragmatics*. (Handbooks of Pragmatics 10). Berlin: de Gruyter, pp. 305–331.

Green, Georgia M. (1989). *Pragmatics and Natural Language Understanding*. Hillsdale, NJ: Lawrence Erlbaum.

Haugh, Michael. (2015). *Im/Politeness Implicatures*. (Mouton Series in Pragmatics). Berlin: de Gruyter.

Haugh, Michael. (2018). Corpus-based metapragmatics. In Andreas H. Jucker, Klaus P. Schneider and Wolfram Bublitz (eds.). *Methods in Pragmatics*. (Handbooks of Pragmatics 10). Berlin: de Gruyter, pp. 619–643.

Haugh, Michael and Wei-Lin Melody Chang. (2019). 'The apology seemed (in) sincere': Variability in perceptions of (im)politeness. *Journal of Pragmatics* 142, 207–222.

Holmes, Janet. (1984). Modifying illocutionary force. *Journal of Pragmatics* 8, 345–365.

Holmes, Janet. (1988). Paying compliments: A sex preferential politeness strategy. *Journal of Pragmatics* 12.4, 445–465.

Holmes, Janet. (1990). Apologies in New Zealand English. *Language in Society* 19.2, 155–199.

Holmes, Janet. (1995). *Women, Men and Politeness*. London: Longman.

House, Juliane, Dániel Z. Kádár, Fengguang Liu and Wenrui Shi. (2023). Historical language use in Europe from a contrastive pragmatic perspective: An exploratory case study of letter closings. *Journal of Historical Pragmatics* 24.1, 143–159.

Hübscher, Iris, Cristina Sánchez-Conde, Joan Borràs-Comes, Laura Vincze and Pilar Prieto. (2023). Multimodal mitigation: How facial and body cues index politeness in Catalan requests. *Journal of Politeness Research* 19.1, 1–29.

Jacobs, Andreas and Andreas H. Jucker. (1995). The historical perspective in pragmatics. In Andreas H. Jucker (ed.). *Historical Pragmatics: Pragmatic Developments in the History of English.* (Pragmatics and Beyond New Series 35). Amsterdam: John Benjamins, pp. 3–33.

Jucker, Andreas H. (2018). Apologies in the history of English: Evidence from the Corpus of Historical American English (COHA). *Corpus Pragmatics* 2.4, 375–398.

Jucker, Andreas H. (2019). Speech act attenuation in the history of English: The case of apologies. *Glossa: A Journal of General Linguistics* 4.1, 45, 1–25.

Jucker, Andreas H. (2023). 'He offered an apologetic smile.' The politeness of apologetic gestures. In Andreas H. Jucker, Iris Hübscher and Lucien Brown (eds.). *Multimodal Im/politeness: Signed, Spoken, Written.* (Pragmatics and Beyond New Series 333). Amsterdam: John Benjamins, pp. 327–351.

Jucker, Andreas H. (in press). 'Is that a request or a command?' Speech act meta discourse and illocutionary indeterminacy. In Niklas Fischer, Steve Oswald, Kilian Schindler and Julia Straub (eds.). *Trust and Uncertainty: Perspectives from Linguistics and Literary Studies.* (SPELL 44). Heidelberg: Winter.

Jucker, Andreas H. and Daniela Landert. (2015). Historical pragmatics and early speech recordings: Diachronic developments in turn-taking and narrative structure in radio talk shows. *Journal of Pragmatics* 79, 22–39.

Jucker, Andreas H., Gerold Schneider, Irma Taavitsainen and Barb Breustedt. (2008). Fishing for compliments: Precision and recall in corpus-linguistic compliment research. In Andreas H. Jucker and Irma Taavitsainen (eds.). *Speech Acts in the History of English.* (Pragmatics and Beyond New Series 176). Amsterdam: John Benjamins, pp. 273–294.

Jucker, Andreas H. and Sara W. Smith. (2003). Reference assignment as a communicative task: Differences between native speakers, ESL- and EFL-speakers. In Ewald Mengel, Hans-Jörg Schmid and Michael Steppat (eds.). *Anglistentag 2002 Bayreuth. Proceedings.* Trier: Wissenschaftlicher Verlag, pp. 401–410.

Jucker, Andreas H., Sara W. Smith and Tanja Lüdge. (2003). Interactive aspects of vagueness in conversation. *Journal of Pragmatics* 35, 1737–1769.

Jucker, Andreas H. and Larssyn Staley. (2017). (Im)politeness and developments in methodology. In Jonathan Culpeper, Michael Haugh and Dániel Kádár (eds.). *The Palgrave Handbook of Linguistic (Im)Politeness.* London: Palgrave, pp. 403–429.

Jucker, Andreas H. and Irma Taavitsainen. (2008). Apologies in the history of English: Routinized and lexicalized expressions of responsibility and regret. In Andreas H. Jucker and Irma Taavitsainen (eds.). *Speech Acts in the History of English*. (Pragmatics and Beyond New Series 176). Amsterdam: John Benjamins, pp. 229–244.

Jucker, Andreas H. and Irma Taavitsainen. (2013). *English Historical Pragmatics*. (Edinburgh Textbooks on the English Language). Edinburgh: Edinburgh University Press.

Jucker, Andreas H. and Irma Taavitsainen. (2014). Complimenting in the history of American English: A metacommunicative expression analysis. In Irma Taavitsainen, Andreas H. Jucker and Jukka Tuominen (eds.). *Diachronic Corpus Pragmatics*. (Pragmatics and Beyond New Series 243). Amsterdam: John Benjamins, pp. 257–276.

Kendon, Adam. (2004). *Gesture: Visible Action as Utterance*. Cambridge: Cambridge University Press.

Kendon, Adam. (2017). Pragmatic functions of gestures: Some observations on the history of their study and their nature. *Gesture* 16.2, 157–175.

Kohnen, Thomas (2007). Text types and the methodology of diachronic speech act analysis. In Susan M. Fitzmaurice and Irma Taavitsainen (eds.). *Methodological Issues in Historical Pragmatics*. Berlin: Mouton de Gruyter, pp. 139–166.

Kohnen, Thomas. (2008). Tracing directives through text and time: Towards a methodology of a corpus-based diachronic speech-act analysis. In Andreas H. Jucker and Irma Taavitsainen (eds.). *Speech Acts in the History of English* (Pragmatics and Beyond New Series 176). Amsterdam: John Benjamins, pp. 295–310.

Kohnen, Thomas. (2015). Speech acts: A diachronic perspective. In Karin Aijmer and Christoph Rühlemann (eds.). *Corpus Pragmatics: A Handbook*. Cambridge: Cambridge University Press, pp. 52–83.

Kohnen, Thomas. (2017). Non-canonical speech acts in the history of English. *Zeitschrift für Anglistik und Amerikanistik* 65.3, 303–318.

Landert, Daniela, Daria Dayter, Thomas C. Messerli and Miriam A. Locher. (2023). *Corpus Pragmatics*. (Cambridge Elements). Cambridge: Cambridge University Press.

Leech, Geoffrey N. (1983). *Principles of Pragmatics*. London: Longman.

Levinson, Stephen C. (1983). *Pragmatics*. Cambridge: Cambridge University Press.

Levinson, Stephen C. (2015). Speech acts. In Yan Huang (ed.). *The Oxford Handbook of Pragmatics*. Oxford: Oxford University Press, pp. 199–216.

Locher, Miriam A. and Andreas H. Jucker. (2021). *The Pragmatics of Fiction: Literature, Stage and Screen Discourse*. Edinburgh: Edinburgh University Press.

Manes, Joan and Nessa Wolfson. (1981). The compliment formula. In Florian Coulmas, (ed.). *Conversational Routine: Explorations in Standardized Communication Situations and Prepatterned Speech*. The Hague: Mouton, pp. 115–132.

Mascuñana, Evelyn F., Myla June T. Patron, Warlito S. Caturay Jr and Hermiesela B. Duran. (2019). Compliment responses by college male and female Filipino second language learners of English. *Corpus Pragmatics* 3: 67–91.

McNeill, David. (2005). *Gesture and Thought*. Chicago, IL: University of Chicago Press.

McNeill, David. (2012). *How Language Began: Gesture and Speech in Human Evolution*. Cambridge: Cambridge University Press.

McNeill, David. (2015). *Why We Gesture: The Surprising Role of Hand Movements in Communication*. Cambridge: Cambridge University Press.

Müller, Cornelia, Alan Cienki, Ellen Fricke, Silva H. Ladewig, David McNeill and Sedinha Teßendorf (eds.). (2013). *Body – Language – Communication: An International Handbook on Multimodality in Human Interaction*. Volume 1 (Handbooks of Linguistics and Communication Science 38.1). Berlin: De Gruyter Mouton.

Müller, Cornelia, Alan Cienki, Ellen Fricke, Silva H. Ladewig, David McNeill and Jana Bressem (eds.). (2014). *Body – Language – Communication: An International Handbook on Multimodality in Human Interaction*. Volume 2 (Handbooks of Linguistics and Communication Science 38.2). Berlin: De Gruyter Mouton.

Murphy, James. (2019). 'I'm sorry you are such an arsehole': (Non-)canonical apologies and their implications for (im)politeness. *Journal of Pragmatics* 142, 223–232.

Nilsson, Jenny, Jan Lindström, Love Bohman, Catrin Norrby, Klara Skogmyr Marian and Camilla Wide. (2022). Pragmatic variation across geographical and social space. In Andreas H. Jucker and Heiko Hausendorf (eds.). *Pragmatics of Space*. (Handbooks of Pragmatics 14). Berlin: De Gruyter Mouton, pp. 611–635.

O'Keeffe, Anne. (2018). Corpus-based function-to-form approaches. In Andreas H. Jucker, Klaus P. Schneider and Wolfram Bublitz (eds.). *Methods in Pragmatics* (Handbooks of Pragmatics 10). Berlin: de Gruyter, pp. 587–618.

Ogierman, Eva. (2018). Discourse completion tasks. In Andreas H. Jucker, Klaus P. Schneider and Wolfram Bublitz (eds.). *Methods in Pragmatics* (Handbooks of Pragmatics 10). Berlin: De Gruyter, pp. 229–255.

Reber, Elisabeth. (2021). *Quoting in Parliamentary Question Time: Exploring Recent Change*. Cambridge: Cambridge University Press.

Reber, Elisabeth and Andreas H. Jucker (eds.). (2023). *Journal of Pragmatics*. VSI *Diachronic Pragmatics*: *Perspectives on Spoken English*. https://www.science direct.com/journal/journal-of-pragmatics/special-issue/10DMQ1HQP05

Rieger, Caroline L. (2017). 'I want a real apology': A discursive pragmatic perspective on apologies. *Pragmatics* 274, 553–590.

Rüegg, Larssyn. (2014). Thanks responses in three socio-economic settings: A variational pragmatics approach. *Journal of Pragmatics* 71, 17–30.

Schegloff, Emanuel A. (2007). *Sequence Organization in Interaction: A Primer in Conversation Analysis I*. Cambridge: Cambridge University Press.

Schneider, Klaus P. (2011). Imagining conversation: How people think people do things with words. *Sociolinguistic Studies* 5.1, 15–36.

Schneider, Klaus P. (2017). Is that a threat? Forms and functions of metapragmatic terms in English discourse. *AAA – Arbeiten aus Anglistik und Amerikanistik* 42.2, 225–242.

Schneider, Klaus P. (2021). Notes on variational metapragmatics. *Journal of Pragmatics* 179, 12–18.

Schneider, Klaus P. (2022). Referring to speech acts in communication: Exploring meta-illocutionary expressions in ICE-Ireland. *Corpus Pragmatics* 6, 1–22.

Schoppa, Dominik Jan. (2022). Conceptualizing illocutions in context: A variationist perspective on the meta-illocutionary lexicon. *Corpus Pragmatics* 6, 63–88.

Searle, John R. (1969). *Speech Acts: An Essay in the Philosophy of Language*. Cambridge: Cambridge University Press.

Searle, John R. (1976). A classification of illocutionary acts. *Language in Society* 5, 1–23.

Searle, John R. (1979). *Expression and Meaning: Studies in the Theory of Speech Acts*. Cambridge: Cambridge University Press.

Staley, Larssyn. (2018). *Socioeconomic Pragmatic Variation: Speech Acts and Address Forms in Context*. (Pragmatics and Beyond New Series 291). Amsterdam: John Benjamins.

Strubel-Burgdorf, Susanne. (2018). *Compliments and Positive Assessments: Sequential Organization in Multi-party Conversations*. (Pragmatics and Beyond New Series 289). Amsterdam: John Benjamins.

Szatrowski, Polly E. (2014). Modality and evidentiality in Japanese and American English taster lunches: Identifying and assessing an unfamiliar drink. In Polly E. Szatrowski (ed.). *Language and Food: Verbal and Nonverbal Experiences*. (Pragmatics and Beyond New Series 238). Amsterdam: John Benjamins, pp. 131–157.

Taavitsainen, Irma and Andreas H. Jucker. (2008). 'Methinks you seem more beautiful than ever': Compliments and gender in the history of English. In Andreas H. Jucker and Irma Taavitsainen (eds.). *Speech Acts in the History of English*. (Pragmatics and Beyond New Series 176). Amsterdam: John Benjamins, pp. 195–228.

Taavitsainen, Irma and Matylda Włodarczyk. (2021). Contrastive pragmatics in a diachronic perspective: Insights from Othello. *Contrastive Pragmatics*, 168–199.

Traugott, Elizabeth Closs. (1991) English speech act verbs: A historical perspective. In Linda R. Waugh and Stephen Rudy (eds.). *New Vistas in Grammar: Invariance and Variation*. Amsterdam: Benjamins, 387–406.

Traugott, Elizabeth Closs. (2008). The state of English language studies: A linguistic perspective. In Marianne Thormählen (ed.). *English Now: Selected Papers from the 20th IAUPE Conference in Lund 2007*. Lund: Lund Studies in English, pp. 199–225.

Traugott, Elizabeth Closs and Richard B. Dasher. (2005). *Regularity in Semantic Change*. Cambridge: Cambridge University Press.

Trosborg, Anna. (1995). *Interlanguage Pragmatics: Requests, Complaints and Apologies*. Berlin: Mouton de Gruyter.

Verschueren, Jef. (1985). What People Say They Do with Words: Prolegomena to an Empirical-Conceptual Approach to Linguistic Action. Norwood, NJ: Ablex.

Verschueren, Jef. (1994). Speech act verbs. In R. E. Asher and J. M. Y. Simpson (eds.). *The Encyclopedia of Language and Linguistics*. Volume 8. Oxford: Pergamon Press, pp. 4138–4140.

Williams, Graham. (2018). *Sincerity in Medieval English Language and Literature*. London: Palgrave Macmillan.

Cambridge Elements ☰

Pragmatics

Jonathan Culpeper
Lancaster University, UK

Jonathan Culpeper is Professor of English Language and Linguistics in the Department of Linguistics and English Language at Lancaster University, UK. A former co-editor-in-chief of the *Journal of Pragmatics* (2009–14), with research spanning multiple areas within pragmatics, his major publications include: *Impoliteness: Using Language to Cause Offence* (2011, CUP) and *Pragmatics and the English Language* (2014, Palgrave; with Michael Haugh).

Michael Haugh
University of Queensland, Australia

Michael Haugh is Professor of Linguistics and Applied Linguistics in the School of Languages and Cultures at the University of Queensland, Australia. A former co-editor-in-chief of the *Journal of Pragmatics* (2015–2020), with research spanning multiple areas within pragmatics, his major publications include: *Understanding Politeness* (2013, CUP; with Dániel Kádár), *Pragmatics and the English Language* (2014, Palgrave; with Jonathan Culpeper), and *Im/politeness Implicatures* (2015, Mouton de Gruyter).

Advisory Board

About the Series

The Cambridge Elements in Pragmatics series showcases dynamic and high-quality original, concise and accessible scholarly works. Written for a broad pragmatics readership it encourages dialogue across different perspectives on language use. It is a forum for cutting-edge work in pragmatics: consolidating theory (especially through cross-fertilization), leading the development of new methods, and advancing innovative topics in pragmatics.

Cambridge Elements ⹀

Pragmatics

Elements in the Series

Advice in Conversation: Corpus Pragmatics Meets Mixed Methods
Nele Põldvere, Rachele De Felice and Carita Paradis

Positive Social Acts: A Metapragmatic Exploration of the Brighter and Darker Sides of Sociability
Roni Danziger

Pragmatics in Translation: Mediality, Participation and Relational Work
Daria Dayter, Miriam A. Locher and Thomas C. Messerli

Corpus Pragmatics
Daniela Landert, Daria Dayter, Thomas C. Messerli and Miriam A. Locher

Fiction and Pragmatics
Miriam A. Locher, Andreas H. Jucker, Daniela Landert and Thomas C. Messerli

Pragmatics, (Im)Politeness, and Intergroup Communication: A Multilayered, Discursive Analysis of Cancel Culture
Pilar G. Blitvich

Pragmatics, Utterance Meaning, and Representational Gesture
Jack Wilson

Leveraging Relations in Diaspora: Occupational Recommendations among Latin Americans in London
Rosina Márquez Reiter

The Dark Matter of Pragmatics: Known Unknowns
Stephen C. Levinson

Pragmatic Inference: Misunderstandings, Accountability, Deniability
Chi-Hé Elder

Speech Acts: Discursive, Multimodal, Diachronic
Andreas H. Jucker

A full series listing is available at: www.cambridge.org/EIPR

Printed in the United States
by Baker & Taylor Publisher Services